THE
DANCER
WHO FLEW

THE DANCER WHO FLEW

A Memoir of Rudolf Nureyev

❧

LINDA MAYBARDUK

TUNDRA BOOKS

Published in Canada by Tundra Books, *McClelland & Stewart Young Readers*, 481 University Avenue, Toronto, Ontario M5G 2E9

Published in the United States by Tundra Books of Northern New York, P.O. Box 1030, Plattsburgh, New York 12901

Library of Congress Catalog Number: 99-70969

Canadian Cataloguing in Publication Data

Maybarduk, Linda
    The dancer who flew : a memoir of Rudolf Nureyev

ISBN 0-88776-415-0

1. Nureyev, Rudolf, 1938-1993 – Juvenile literature. 2. Ballet dancers – Russia (Federation) – Biography – Juvenile literature. I. Title.

GV1785.N8M39 1999   j792.8028092   C99-930613-8

We acknowledge the support of the Canada Council for the Arts and the Ontario Arts Council for our publishing program.

We acknowledge the financial support of the Government of Canada through the Book Publishing Industry Development Program for our publishing activities.

Canadä

Design by Sari Ginsberg

Printed and bound in Canada

1 2 3 4 5 6   04 03 02 01 00 99

To my parents, who always stood by me with love and support in my career as a dancer

To my family, who provided me with love and encouragement during the writing of this book

And to Rudolf . . . a promise kept

— L.M.

CONTENTS

Rossi Street, St. Petersburg.

BACKGROUND

Russia has had a long and tumultuous history, and this past century, roughly the period covered in this book, has been one of its most turbulent. During this time, the country has gone from being a monarchy to a Communist federation to an independent state.

All of this political turmoil has also meant numerous changes in geographical names. For example, St. Petersburg, which was originally named for Peter the Great and is the city where much of this book's story takes place, was rechristened Petrograd (1914-24) and then, after the death of Vladimir Ilyich Lenin, the leader of the Russian Revolution, changed again to Leningrad (1924-91). In 1991, with the birth of the Commonwealth of Independent States, the name St. Petersburg was restored. Other Russian cities and towns have undergone similar changes.

This political instability affected even the names of many organizations and institutions, including the ballet school Rudolf Nureyev attended. Throughout its long history, it has been known variously as the Maryinsky School, the Leningrad Ballet School, the Kirov School, and the Vaganova Ballet Academy.

To avoid confusion, we have tried to be consistent in our use of names, and have usually opted for the term that Nureyev himself would have used. Thus, the city is referred to as Leningrad, the school as the Leningrad Ballet School, and the ballet company and the building in which the company performed as the Kirov. Terms within quotations have been unchanged, as they reflect the reality of the past.

introduction

The first time I saw Rudolf Nureyev dance, he took my breath away. It was a January evening in 1962, and I was eleven years old. Along with millions of other viewers, I saw him make his North American debut on the NBC television program "The Bell Telephone Hour." His partner was one of America's greatest ballerinas, Maria Tallchief.

I can still picture myself: a young ballet student kneeling in front of the TV, my back ramrod straight, my heart quickening with excitement. After the show, I literally danced down the corridor to my room and made a flying leap into bed. Snuggling under the covers, I tried to imagine all kinds of wonderful situations that would allow me to dance someday with Rudolf Nureyev. That night, a dream was born in me.

Over the next few years, his achievements fed my own ambition to become a ballerina. When I was fifteen, I finally saw him dance in a live performance. It was May 1965. My parents had taken me to Washington, D.C., from our hometown of Orlando, Florida, to meet up with England's Royal Ballet, which was then touring the United States. I was to audition for the illustrious Royal Ballet School in front of Michael Somes, a former premier danseur who was now the assistant director of the company. Immediately after my audition, Somes told me that I had been accepted! And more good news followed. He offered me and my parents three tickets for that day's matinee and evening performances.

The Royal Ballet was — and still is — one of the world's greatest ballet companies. I had read about all of its stars, and I had collected many of

Rudolf and the author rehearsing in a studio at the Metropolitan Opera House in New York City in 1975.

their pictures and taped them to my bedroom wall. In that afternoon's production, I was lucky enough to see a dozen of them perform live. They all danced more beautifully than I had ever imagined. But I knew that even more thrilling moments were to come in the evening's performance — Nureyev was scheduled to dance in his own version of *La Bayadère.*

After the matinee, my parents and I waited backstage for Somes to give us our tickets for the evening program. He was in a hurry; he had to speak with Nureyev before the show. Almost as an afterthought, he asked me if I would like to meet the famous dancer. The expression on my face said it all, and Somes invited us to follow him. At the dressing-room door, Somes conferred with the superstar about some future rehearsals. When he concluded his business, he introduced my parents and then explained that I had just been accepted into the Royal Ballet School. Rudolf invited us into his dressing room.

In all my fantasies about meeting the star, I had pictured myself as a poised and intelligent young woman. Unfortunately, the moment he reached out to shake my hand and congratulate me, I dissolved into a flood of tears. I was so overcome that I can no longer recall the words Rudolf said to me. All I can remember is his kind and enthusiastic smile, a pat on the shoulder, and his general comments of congratulations and encouragement. Alas, it was my father who was the beneficiary of a wonderful fifteen-minute conversation, all in Russian, with my idol.

Luckily, my tears had not rendered me blind. Everything I had read about Nureyev — and I had read everything — made him seem larger than life, so I was surprised to find that he was of only medium build and height. Our intrusion into his dressing room had obviously disturbed his preparations for the stage. His makeup was not yet complete, and his long, light brown hair was tousled and uncombed; it looked not unlike a lion's mane, and had the effect of softening the chiseled features of his face. The shading of his makeup accentuated his already prominent cheekbones and full lips. There was a distinct scar above his lip, which, I would learn in later years, he had acquired in childhood, when he was bitten by a neighbor's dog. But his eyes were his most remarkable feature. Brimming with expression, they drew you in like a magnet. When he laughed, they twinkled with genuine pleasure, and when he spoke seriously, they were earnest and intense.

In all too short a time, our meeting ended. Rudolf needed to prepare for his performance, and we needed to find our seats in the audience. We watched the first two ballets of the evening with the same excitement we had felt in the matinee. As the curtain went up for the last ballet, *La Bayadère*, my heart was pounding in anticipation of Rudolf's entrance. Suddenly, he appeared, running from the wings like a fiery comet. The sheer energy of his entrance electrified us, and the audience exploded in tumultuous applause. Like everyone else in that vast auditorium, I was seized by the moment. Once again, Rudolf had taken my breath away.

Six years passed before I met Rudolf Nureyev again. By that time, I had graduated from Canada's National Ballet School (which, for a variety of reasons, I had ended up attending instead of the Royal Ballet School), and I was a first soloist with the National Ballet of Canada. Rudolf came to dance with the company in the late summer of 1972. Time had not diminished my admiration for him, but a little maturity on my part ensured that I did not embarrass myself again. Better still, I learned that I had been cast to dance a pas de deux with him in Erik Bruhn's production of *Swan Lake.* Thanks to a little good luck and a decade of hard work, my dream of dancing with Rudolf was about to come true.

In September, the evening of our first performance finally arrived. When it was our turn to dance, Rudolf extended his hand to me in a princely invitation to begin our pas de deux. Sensing my nervousness, he looked me straight in the eyes, commanding me to be brave. I can still conjure up the mixture of excitement, pride, and nervousness I felt as we promenaded in a grand circle to take our places. Just before we turned to face the audience, Rudolf gave my hand a quick squeeze for reassurance. And then we danced. The long-awaited moment was even more thrilling than I had imagined it would be.

As time went by, my own relationship with Rudolf evolved. We danced together for many years and in many ballets. He became not only my teacher and partner, but also my mentor and friend. He offered advice and made opportunities for me. When I married, his friendship extended to my husband, Bill, and my relationship with Rudolf took on a more equal and adult footing. When I retired, and after I gave birth to my first child, Michael, Rudolf adopted us as his "Toronto family." As with the other families Rudolf adopted in cities around the world, he often stayed with us, eventually becoming a favorite uncle to our sons, Michael and Cameron, and a godfather to our daughter, Alexandra.

Rudolf Nureyev changed the lives of all who knew him. A talent of his magnitude is seen not more than a few times in a century, and it was a blessing beyond words to have played a small professional and personal role in his extraordinary life. He showed those of us who were fortunate enough to have shared a stage with him the pinnacle of our profession, teaching us not only with his words, but also by example. My purpose in writing this book is to pass on some of the many things Rudolf generously taught me — as both a dancer and a friend.

Of course, Rudolf's life was not without controversy. His personal relationships were complex and at times tumultuous, and his explosive Tatar temper was legendary. But *The Dancer Who Flew* is not a tell-all about his private life; it is a professional memoir of the ballet star as remembered by a fellow dancer and a friend. This book is intended to look at Rudolf's impact as an artist, as a dancer, and as an influential creative genius.

As one of the twentieth century's greatest artists and best-known celebrities, Rudolf Nureyev came to symbolize dance in much the same way as Babe Ruth symbolizes baseball and Luciano Pavarotti does the opera. He was a force in the dance world, and his contributions were enormous and revolutionary. His superior talent and charismatic presence drew millions of people to the ballet for the first time, creating a worldwide audience for dance. His technical prowess and masculine style made dancing once again an acceptable profession for men. By his own example, he raised the standards of the art form throughout the world, and he inspired several generations of younger dancers to follow in his footsteps. But his pioneering effort to bring together ballet and American modern dance may stand as his greatest contribution. It is no wonder that those in the dance world referred to him as "the God of Dance" — a title that, historically, has been bestowed on just a few. In the twentieth century, he shared it with only Vaslav Nijinsky.

Rudolf was a ferociously curious and brave artist. Inside his own profession, he not only danced but also choreographed and directed. Outside dance, he tried other art forms, such as acting in motion pictures and on the musical-theater stage, often risking criticism and ridicule. At the end of his life, he even became a symphony conductor. But in his heart, nothing ever replaced the pure physical pleasure he felt from dancing. From the moment he saw his first ballet in the opera house in his industrial hometown of Ufa, Russia, he was consumed by a love for dance and the burning desire to be on a stage. With the very first steps he took with a school folk-dance troupe, he found his heart's desire. Toward the end of his career, Rudolf would best sum up his life: "In all my life, there has just been one love — dancing. I couldn't live without dance. When you watch me dance, you see real me. I was born to be on stage, and I daresay it shows."

This is his story.

BORN IN MOTION

I must be a dancer. I will be a dancer.
— Rudolf Nureyev, age seven

Rudolf Nureyev was literally born in motion. His mother, Farida, was traveling on the Trans-Siberian Railroad with her three young daughters, Rosa, Lilya, and Razida, from her home in Russia's Ural region to the far-eastern port city of Vladivostok, almost a week away. Her husband, Hamet, who was in the Red Army, had been stationed at the remote seaport to instruct a regiment of soldiers in the political teachings of Communism. Although she was eight months pregnant, Farida made the arduous journey over the vast and snowy landscape because she wanted to reunite her family before the new baby was born. But on March 17, 1938, as the train rocked past the shores of Lake Baikal, still nineteen hundred miles (more than 3,000 km) from its destination, the Nureyevs' only son made an early appearance.

The boy was born at one of the most horrific periods of the century. Only twenty-one years earlier, in 1917, Tsar Nicholas II had been overthrown in a bloody revolution by Vladimir Ilyich Lenin, the leader of a Russian political party known as the Bolsheviks. In 1918, Lenin became the first premier of a new federation of Communist states that would

Rudolf — or Rudik, as his family called him — around age five, with a toy pistol.

eventually be called the Union of Soviet Socialist Republics, or the Soviet Union. The early principles of Communism had come from the writings of the German political philosopher Karl Marx, who envisioned a society in which all people would be treated equally. For many in Russia, where a handful of citizens enjoyed every privilege while millions of others were close to starvation, Communism seemed to offer great hope. But in practice, it was not the ideal of which people had dreamed. Indeed, Lenin and his successor, Joseph Stalin, were dictators who controlled the country through force and cruelty.

At the time of Rudolf's birth, war clouds were gathering in Europe, and Russia was gripped by what would become known as the Great Terror or the Great Purge. This terrible period began in 1934 with the assassination of a Communist Party leader, Sergei Kirov. To honor the memory of his slain comrade, Stalin renamed Leningrad's ballet company after Kirov and then unleashed a nationwide reign of terror in his search for real and imagined traitors. No one was safe. Many millions of people were either executed or sent to labor camps in Siberia, and even today there is no exact record of how many perished. Throughout the Soviet Union, people were rewarded for reporting on friends or family members who spoke against the government or acted suspiciously. Even children were encouraged to turn in their parents for any perceived disloyalty to the party. And escape? Leaving Russia without official permission was also considered an act of treason, and was punishable by a long prison term or death.

Under Communism, personal freedom was also limited in other ways. No one was allowed to own property, for instance, and religion was banned. But most loyal Communists, like the Nureyevs, did not object to any of this. Although they were Muslim Tatars, and were descended from the Mongols who had conquered Russia under Genghis Khan in the thirteenth century, the Nureyevs turned their backs on their faith when the revolution swept the country.

Yet despite the terrors imposed by the state, daily life improved for many people in the Soviet Union. Rudolf's parents, like many other Russians, embraced the new political system. They had come from peasant families who had known backbreaking work in the fields before the revolution, and they believed that Communism would give their children opportunities they themselves had been denied.

Rudolf's family remained in a town north of Vladivostok for a year and a half. When Hamet was reassigned to the capital city of Moscow, the family boarded the Trans-Siberian Express once again to travel back across the immense Russian continent. For Hamet, an ambitious and dedicated Communist, the transfer was important because it put him at the very center of power. Farida was pleased, too, for their daughter Lilya was nearly deaf, and in Moscow there would be special schools for her.

By this time, the horrors of the Second World War had already begun to be experienced in Europe, but the family felt safe in Moscow. Thanks to Hamet's Communist connections, the Nureyevs lived comfortably in a small apartment. In 1941, however, their relatively secure life changed abruptly when Adolf Hitler's German army launched a surprise attack on Russia, and the country was plunged into war. Rudolf was only three when his father was sent to the battlefront. Fearing the bombs and an invasion of Moscow, Farida decided she had to evacuate her family to safety. It was a race for survival. She packed up the few belongings she could push in a wheelbarrow, and once again the family set out on a journey. Rudolf recalled later in life, in his characteristic halting English, "I remember sitting on a wheelbarrow with tea kettle swinging back and forth as we hurried to train." They fled to their ancestral province, Bashkir.

At first, the family took refuge in the village of Tchichuna. Rudolf, his three older sisters, and his mother were allotted living space in a small, crude cabin that already housed other families. Years later, Rudolf

This izba, or peasant hut, is like the one the Nureyevs shared with other families in Tchichuna.

would tell me, "I still remember the cold awakenings on dark winter mornings, and lack of privacy. I was an energetic child, with an active imagination, so worse than crowding was the numbing boredom of long, lonely days trapped inside, with little to excite my imagination."

Among those sharing the cabin was an elderly Christian couple. Unlike Rudolf's parents, who as ardent Communists frowned on religious worship, the older people continued to devoutly follow their faith. In spite of Farida's strong disapproval, they even tried to convert her impressionable young son. "They promised me an extra ration of food if I would join them in their early morning prayers," he recalled. "It was dark and I was very sleepy — but more hungry than sleepy. My mother disapproved, but even at such a young age I defied her. Every morning at dawn I knelt on bare, dirt floor and prayed in front of their icons, because those morsels helped pain in my empty stomach. My one lasting memory of early childhood is of throbbing hunger."

In 1943, Hamet's brother, Nurislam, invited Farida and the children to live with his family in Bashkir's capital, Ufa. Ufa is situated on the

Left: Rudolf as a child with his sisters, Razida, Lilya, and Rosa. This picture was taken during the Second World War, and their shabby clothes attest to the toll the war took on many Russian families. Right: Rudolf's mother, Farida. "As a child, I rarely saw my mother smile," he once said of her.

Belaya River, near the rich mineral resources of the Ural Mountains. During the Second World War, the city was a center for defense and heavy industry, as well as for oil and gas refineries. It was also a place of deadly secrecy. So mysterious was Ufa, in fact, that it was often deliberately removed from or marked incorrectly on official Soviet maps.

Rudolf's mother and sisters thought their living conditions in Ufa — they shared space in a barracks-like building with their uncle's family — were somewhat better than they had been in Tchichuna. When Rudolf spoke about this period in his life, however, he remembered the cramped quarters as "nightmarish." Hunger and deprivation were recurring themes in the stories he told about his early years in Ufa.

One story he often repeated involved his mother's setting out for a village eighteen miles (30 km) away to trade her husband's civilian clothes for food. Forced to make her journey in the depths of winter, Farida wrapped an extra blanket around her shoulders for warmth and headed off. But where the road cut through a deep forest, she heard noises behind her. Turning around, she caught the glint of eyes gazing at her through the trees. Starving wolves were stalking her. Terrified, Farida pulled off the blanket and set it on fire. Waving the blazing cloth frantically in the air, she frightened the wolves away and saved herself. Whenever he told the story, Rudolf spoke proudly of his mother's great bravery and resourcefulness. "When others would have given up or perished, she stood her ground," he would say. "Throughout my life, I have tried to follow her example."

Although he was small for his age, Rudolf was a handsome child with blond hair, green eyes, and the high cheekbones of his Tatar ancestors. His sisters and his mother called him Rudik and doted on the baby of the family. He was always in motion, running, twirling, or jumping. Even on rainy days, when Ufa's streets turned to mud, Rudolf would run outside, jump over puddles, push his young muscles to propel him higher and farther. He must have been a handful for his sisters, who, with their father away at war and their mother working long days in a factory, were often left to care for him alone.

In the evenings, the children joined their mother in the communal kitchen of the crowded house to eat their meager dinner. Often, it consisted of no more than potatoes. Afterward, they would return to their own room to listen to the family's prized possession, a radio, one of the few belongings Farida had brought with them when they fled Moscow. In his autobiography, Rudolf wrote: "I would sit by it, quite still, for hours, listening to the music, any kind of music. All that I knew was that somehow, through music, I could escape from the room with its ten inhabitants, escape from my lonely childhood. I looked upon music, from my earliest days, as a friend, a religion, a way to good fortune."

At bedtime, Rudolf's preferred way to fall asleep was to listen to his mother tell him his favorite folktales. He also enjoyed snuggling under the bedcovers as Rosa and Razida read him fairy tales and the stories of Jules Verne, who wrote *Twenty Thousand Leagues under the Sea* and *Around the World in Eighty Days*. Later in life, Rudolf told many of his friends that he believed his longing to travel and see the wider world first came from listening to the tales of Verne. This nighttime ritual also sparked a lifelong passion for reading, a habit that stimulated his already well-developed imagination.

By this time, Rudolf was old enough to spend full days in school. Sadly, the world beyond the safe circle of his sisters and mother proved to be a miserable place. For one thing, the family was so poor that he owned no shoes (on his first day, his mother carried him across the street to school on her back), and his sister's hand-me-down cape, complete with wings, served as his coat. The other children teased him because of his shabby clothes — girls' clothes — and called him a beggar. Worse yet, Rudolf was an unusual name in Russia (according to Nureyev, his mother had named him after her movie idol, Rudolph Valentino). The other children tormented the boy by calling him Adolf, after Adolf Hitler, the hated German dictator who was waging war against their country.

Although more recent biographies speak about his childhood friends, Rudolf himself always described his early years to me as solitary and isolated. He saw himself as a loner and a misfit. Music was his chief refuge, he said, and his imagination saved him from his unhappy life at school. He once described to me a hill near his home where he sometimes took sanctuary. From his "private observation post," as he called it, he'd spend hours watching the trains enter and leave the local station. He enjoyed feeling their rhythm, their power, and their speed. While dreaming and pondering his future, he longed for the day when one of those mighty machines would carry him far away from his drab life in Ufa.

When Rudolf was seven, a single event changed his life forever. It was New Year's Eve, 1945, and a gala ballet performance was to take place at the Ufa Opera House.

Although much of life in Stalin's USSR was harsh, many Soviets retained a passionate love for the arts. Ballet, music, and poetry were treasured, and provided a way for people to transport themselves from the hard realities of hunger, oppression, and war. So it was only natural that a factory worker like Farida Nureyev would know about the upcoming gala. She desperately wanted to take her children, but since she barely had enough money to keep food on the table, buying five tickets was an impossibility. She could afford only one.

On the day of the performance, Farida hurried her children through the snowy streets to the opera house. They went early so she could come up with a plan to smuggle in her whole family, but a crowd had already gathered and was pushing at the front doors to be let in. "As a small child, it was frightening for me," Rudolf remembered. "People jostled and elbowed each other, and screamed for doors to be opened. All the confusion worried my mother, and she told us to hold on tightly to her and to each other." Suddenly, the crush of the mob forced the doors of the theater to swing open. The Nureyevs were swept into the opera house without anyone checking their tickets. Luckily, Farida's seat was in a box high over the orchestra. She quickly pushed her whole family in, and no one noticed that they had only one ticket.

"I squirmed to front of box to get my first look at such a magical place. Peering out over audience, it seemed to me like a fairy-tale palace — all gold and velvet," Rudolf later recalled. "There were shimmering crystal chandeliers, lanterns with soft light; and below, musicians warmed up with their instruments. It was so beautiful! So enchanting! At that moment, I felt transported to another world."

He told himself that he must try to remember every single detail of this wonderful evening. The lights dimmed in the theater, the conductor entered the illuminated orchestra pit, and members of the audience started to clap their hands. (Years later, Rudolf would say he was utterly intrigued that the audience applauded before even a note of music had been played or a single step had been danced.) Then the music began. The heavy velvet curtain parted to reveal yet another fairyland on the stage, and the dancers started to perform *The Song of the Cranes,* a new ballet created during the war. It was set in Bashkir and told the story of a shepherd boy's efforts to defeat a cruel rich man for the hand of a maiden. To young Rudolf, the dancers seemed like gods. And the ballerina! How she could leap across the stage. How she could hold such beautiful positions without moving. Her name was Zaituna Nazredinova, and he thought she had to be the greatest ballerina in the world.

"I sat motionless with eyes fixed on stage. I wanted to be on that stage with those dancers! I kept saying to myself, 'I must be a dancer. I will be a dancer.' I remember holding tightly to balcony railing and feeling my nails dig deeply into railing. I was utterly possessed," he recalled. "From that day, I can truly date my unwavering decision to become a ballet dancer. I felt 'called.' Watching the dancers that night, admiring their other-worldly ability to defy the laws of balance and gravity, I had the absolute certitude that I had been born to dance."

Once again, and with great difficulty, Farida had fed her hungry child. This time, it was with ambition and a dream.

2

THE ROAD TO ROSSI STREET

Child, you have a duty to yourself to learn classical dancing!
— Anna Udeltsova, Nureyev's first ballet teacher

All types of traditional folk art — music, painting, embroidery, and especially dancing — have always been held in high regard in Russia. The legendary ballerina Anna Pavlova once said, "You wonder why it is that so many famous dancers have come from Russia and why the art of the ballet developed so wonderfully in my country. The reason is that dancing is instinctive with the Russian. Go into a village on a fête day and you will see the peasants dancing, not with rude, clumsy movements, but dancing with enthusiasm and abandon and grace. The Russians are natural dancers. . . . "

Like so many children in Russia, Rudolf was introduced to the art form through folk-dancing classes at school. The lively routines full of intricate patterns delighted him, and he soaked up every step he was taught. From the beginning, his teachers could see that he had a superb memory for the steps and a natural ability to execute them. Soon he was chosen for the school's folk-dancing troupe. At home each night, listening to the radio, he repeated the troupe's routines over and over again, and tried to find new ways to move. At times, he felt frustrated and con-

Rudolf, when he was about sixteen, working at the barre in Ufa. Notice the struggle for perfection in the expression on his face as he examines his reflection in a mirror.

Rudolf practicing a Bashkiri folk dance.
"When I think back on my childhood,
my only happy times were when
I was dancing."

fined because he did not know enough steps to help him express his intense feelings for the music he heard.

Rudolf shared his love of dancing and music with his sister Rosa, who was ten years older and was studying to be a teacher. "Rosa understood my passions because she, too, was very musical. She helped me by reading books about the history of dance, and almost every night after dinner we sat huddled together, listening to the radio." Farida also recognized her son's musicality and his natural ability. Friends suggested that with his talent, he should be sent to study at the Maryinsky School, the great ballet school in Leningrad (or St. Petersburg, as it is now known). But Leningrad was half a continent away from Ufa, and where would the money come from? It seemed an impossible dream, but it had planted itself in Rudolf's heart.

Hamet, Rudolf's father, during the war. "There was always tension between my father and me," Rudolf explained. "He simply could not understand my need to become a dancer."

Although the Second World War ended in Europe in May 1945, Hamet was not able to return home to his family until August 1946. For five years, Rudolf had enjoyed being the only male in a household of women. When his father eventually returned, a virtual stranger to his children, everything changed.

Hamet had never been a warm man, and unfortunately the long years in battle at the Russian front had served to harden him further. Nevertheless, all through the war he had looked forward to coming home to his family. He especially wanted to spend time with his only son, sharing the pleasures of hunting and fishing. He even acquired a hunting dog for the purpose.

Rudolf's memory of their first hunting trip together was painful. "On our first outing, my father became annoyed that I couldn't walk fast

Rudolf and his family looking more prosperous after Hamet's return from the war.

enough to keep up with him and our dog. So he left me in a rucksack, hanging from tree. I was terrified. I thought I heard animals nearby, my imagination ran wild. I don't remember how long I was there alone. It seemed like hours. I started to cry and call, 'Papa, Papa, I'm frightened! Papa, where are you? Take me home!'" Hamet was furious with his young son and called him a coward. Later, when Rudolf related the story to Farida, she raged at her husband for leaving the child alone and expecting him to be as brave as a man. "My mother never forgave him for that day," Rudolf remembered.

Of course, certain aspects of their lives did improve with Hamet's return. His new civilian job brought in some much-needed income, for one thing, and the Nureyevs were assigned a new flat of their own in a one-story house. But the apartment, although slightly larger than their other wartime homes, still lacked running water. Even in the dead of winter, with their teeth chattering, they had to use an outhouse, and once a week they all made a trip to the local steam bath.

Despite Hamet's added income, poverty remained a concern. Rudolf once told me, for instance, that as a young boy he did not even have his own bed to sleep in. One night, while helping me put my own little boys to sleep, he turned to me in the dark and whispered, "Ah, what a nice room they have. You know, when I was a boy, I had only bench to sleep on and dog's tail for pillow."

As Rudolf grew older, the tension between him and his father mounted. Hamet disapproved of Rudolf's involvement in dancing, and this put a further strain on their relationship. When Rudolf started spending so much time dancing that his grades began to suffer, Hamet became furious with his son and at times beat him. In his autobiography, Rudolf wrote, "He simply could not understand how I could want to become a dancer when I had the chance (which no one in our family had before) of becoming a doctor or engineer."

In an effort to distract his son from his dancing, Hamet enrolled Rudolf in the Young Pioneers, an organization like the Scouts that also taught Russian children about Communism. Hamet believed the group would toughen up the boy and teach him the political principles he himself held so dear. At first, Rudolf hated the idea; but then he met the Pioneers' folk-dance teacher and realized that he would be able to join an additional dance troupe. This troupe gave him new dances and steps to learn, and more opportunities to perform in festivals and for local organizations. His father's plan had backfired.

Once again, Rudolf proved to have a natural gift, not only for the fiery athleticism of the Bashkiri and Tatar dances, but also when he performed to the melodious music of the more fluid folk dances. In fact, the troupe's dance teacher was so impressed by his talent that she introduced him to his first classical ballet teacher, Anna Udeltsova.

Given the Russian passion for the arts, it was not surprising to find gifted ballet dancers even in an industrial town like Ufa. Many creative people had also been exiled to distant provinces like Bashkir both during and after the Russian Revolution, or had fled there for their own safety during the Second World War. Anna Udeltsova was one. She had been a member of the corps de ballet (the dancers in a ballet company who perform as a group and not as soloists) of the famous Ballets Russes of Serge Diaghilev. Rudolf was eleven when she first asked him to demonstrate his folk-dancing solos for her. When he'd finished performing, she proclaimed, "Child, you have a duty to yourself to learn classical dancing! With such an innate gift, you must join the students of the Maryinsky Theater."

Rudolf wanted to start studying with Udeltsova right away, but he knew that his father would not give him money for lessons. Fortunately, the teacher was so impressed by his ability that she invited him to take two classes a week with her at no charge. So Hamet would not find out, Rudolf made excuses to leave the house and used his errand to fetch the family's bread as a cover for attending his ballet classes.

After only a year, Udeltsova felt that she had taught this gifted boy all she could. She handed him over to her more experienced friend, Elena Vaitovitch, who was also an exile from Leningrad. "She was a very good teacher," Rudolf remembered, "and she gave me my first chance to perform a ballet on a stage. Udeltsova and Vaitovitch fed my ambition with stories about life in Leningrad, and they gave me firsthand knowledge of what it could be like in a ballet company. They opened up my provincial eyes. I will always be grateful to them."

Rudolf was making good progress with Vaitovitch when a thrilling announcement came from the Ufa Opera House. A group of children would be selected from the province of Bashkir to audition for the famous Leningrad Ballet School. Here was Rudolf's chance. He pleaded with his father to help him find out how he could take part in the auditions, but Hamet refused. By the time the determined Rudolf was able to convince him, it was too late. The children had left for Leningrad without him.

Rudolf was heartbroken.

Rudolf's dream of the great ballet school was put on hold, but his determination to dance was not. He continued to take his classical ballet classes, and also began to tour with his folk-dance troupe. In fact, he later said that those were his only happy times in those years. "Those folk-dancing performances were wildly improvised," he remembered. "We drove at night from village to village, all our theatrical staff and equipment jammed together into two small trucks. When we stopped, trucks themselves became the stage. Their sides were removed and a wooden floor slung across them both. It makes me smile now when I think how only three years before I was to dance on most beautiful stage in the world, I performed improvised dances on a refurbished truck lit by kerosene lamps."

In one performance, Rudolf was supposed to wear the first costume ever made personally for him, a sailor's uniform. The navy blue pants were not finished on time, so he borrowed a pair from another dancer. But he was so thin that when he was in mid-step, the pants fell down around his ankles. The audience roared with laughter. "It was the funniest performance I ever gave, and the most painful," he once said.

Those early, crude tours in the countryside gave Rudolf invaluable stage experience and taught him many lessons about performing in front of an audience, including how to make the best of the unexpected disasters that sometimes occur on stage. Once, he was to perform with a pole draped with long, trailing ribbons. "Somehow the pole got stuck in stage curtain," he recalled. "I was caught like an animal, completely wrapped up in curtain and ribbons. I felt ridiculous. But I decided to stop the dance and pretend that this was really the climax. Somehow, it worked! Audience cheered and I learned important lesson about doing everything with utmost conviction."

These experiences also showed Rudolf the power that comes from being a performer. His impoverished early years had left him with a feeling of helplessness. But he learned quickly that by dancing a few steps in front of family and friends, or by performing with his school's dance troupe, he could bring himself attention and respect. His dancing made him feel that he had some control, not only in his own life, but also over others.

This overwhelming need to control his own circumstances would become a central part of his character and would shape much of his personality. Indeed, Rudolf often advised, and occasionally ordered, his younger colleagues to follow his example. "Never trust others to do things for you," he said, driving that life lesson into us many times and over many years. "If something needs to be done, do it yourself. You must rely only on yourself."

It was this self-reliance, Rudolf knew, that would take him to Leningrad. Clearly, he could not count on his father, and although his mother, his sister Rosa, and his ballet teachers wanted to help him, they did not have the means. He would have to make his way to Leningrad on his talent, his dedication, and whatever money he could earn.

Taking matters into his own hands, he wrote to the famous ballet school and asked to be allowed to audition for a student scholarship. He waited eagerly, but slowly the weeks turned to months and no reply came.

In the meantime, the sixteen-year-old was invited to perform a walk-on part at the Ufa Opera House. That small role was a turning point for him. For the first time, he was going to appear on a real opera-house stage, and what's more, he would earn ten rubles an evening. He'd also begun to give weekly lessons to local factory workers. Although Hamet was still scornful of Rudolf's desire to dance, he grudgingly admitted that his son was beginning to earn his keep.

Despite his lack of formal training, other small roles came Rudolf's way. Within a year, his success onstage brought him an offer to join the Ufa company as a member of the corps de ballet. But he turned it down. He had finally received a letter from the Leningrad Ballet School. If he could make his way there, an audition awaited him. He knew he was taking an enormous gamble turning down the offer from the Ufa Ballet – it was a solid promise of a career with a highly regarded company, and there were no guarantees that his audition in Leningrad would be successful. However, as he explained, "All I could think of was Leningrad."

Soon after making his decision, Rudolf heard that the provincial culture minister was auditioning dancers to appear in an event in Moscow called "A Decade of Bashkir Art." Rudolf auditioned and was chosen. Moscow was not Leningrad, but it was one step closer to his dream.

While the company was in Moscow, the group's pianist arranged for Rudolf to take classes at the world-famous Bolshoi Ballet. The Bolshoi's teacher was so impressed by Rudolf's raw talent that he immediately offered the teenager a place in the school. Once again, Rudolf turned down a brilliant opportunity. Leningrad was still his goal.

The invitation to join the Bolshoi school gave Rudolf confidence, however, and he decided to use the money he'd earned dancing with the Bashkiris to buy a train ticket to Leningrad. That train trip, as he remembered it years later, was an ordeal. "I had waited for so long time for opportunity. I tried not to ask myself, 'What happens if I fail?' My nerves were in terrible state. The whole journey from Moscow to Leningrad, I stood in the hallway of train. Sixteen hours! There were no

"Even as a child, I knew how to command a stage and I knew how to shine."

seats. By the time I reached Leningrad, I was utterly exhausted. Few times have I ever felt so lonely, so alone, so lost."

But his fatigue was forgotten the minute the train pulled into the station. It had barely stopped moving when Rudolf jumped off, and he dashed straight to the famous school on Rossi Street. "On that Ulitsa Rossi [Rossi Street] almost all the great names of the Russian Ballet started their careers: Pavlova, Nijinsky, Karsavina, Kschessinskaya, Guerdt, Yermolaev, Chabukiani and Balanchine . . . all of them ran to class along that beautiful street. On my first visit there I could hear plainly the echoes of all my idols' footsteps."

Rudolf had arrived when the school was still officially closed for the summer holidays. Nevertheless, he walked the quiet corridors, searching for the director of the school, Valentin Shelkov. When he found the

THE DANCER WHO FLEW

The famous Rossi Street. The Leningrad Ballet School is on the right-hand side. "All the great names of the Russian Ballet . . . ran to class along that beautiful street," wrote Rudolf in his autobiography.

man, he summoned all his courage to introduce himself and ask for an audition. The director set the audition date for a week later.

Luckily, Anna Udeltsova, Rudolf's former teacher from Ufa, was visiting her daughter in Leningrad, and the two women found him a place to stay. Although he was nervous about the upcoming audition, that did not stop him from exploring the wonderful city he had so longed to see. Leningrad still showed the ravages of the Second World War, which had ended only ten years earlier. The Germans had laid siege to the city for nine hundred days, and during that period it is estimated that more than one million people died — many from starvation. The destruction of war and the bleakness of Communism had drained much of the life out of the majestic old city, but what had been spared was still wonderful.

Rudolf ambled along the streets all day and into the summer-lit northern evenings. Strolling across the city's ornate bridges, the teenager paused to admire the classical and baroque buildings that stood majestically along the rivers and canals and reflected their pastel colors in the waters below. He visited the Hermitage Museum (one of the world's most highly regarded art museums), the onion-domed cathedrals, and what was for him the most sacred shrine of them all, the Kirov Theater. If Leningrad was the artistic capital of Russia, then the Kirov Theater was, at least to Rudolf, its crown jewel.

His explorations never left him tired. On the contrary, he drew energy from the beauty around him. He would sit up late into the night, entranced as Udeltsova told him stories of the old days in Russia before Communism. He especially enjoyed hearing her memories of the many legendary dancers she had met during her days in Serge Diaghilev's Ballets Russes. Diaghilev — one of ballet's most important impresarios — had created the Ballets Russes by bringing together some of the greatest dancers, composers, artists, and choreographers of the day. Rudolf asked Udeltsova countless questions about the composer Igor Stravinsky, about the scenic designers Alexander Benois and Léon Bakst, and about the great Diaghilev himself. While listening to her stories, he tried to imagine what it must have been like to perform with the Ballet Russes during the golden age of dance.

But it was the stories about Anna Pavlova and Vaslav Nijinsky that especially thrilled him. They both danced during the very early part of the twentieth century, in the days before motion-picture cameras were in common use, and so no films of Nijinsky's dancing and only a few of Pavlova's survive. Their dancing is kept alive only through photos and descriptions of their art, handed down from dancer to dancer as a precious legacy.

Rudolf was spellbound by Udeltsova's descriptions of how Pavlova and Nijinsky captivated their audiences. She evoked Nijinsky's physical power and haunting stage presence, and Pavlova's passionate dedication. Devouring Udeltsova's words, Rudolf vowed to dedicate himself to his art in the same manner. He particularly felt a kinship with Nijinsky. He liked to point out that they were born under the same astrological sign, Pisces, and he would spend long hours studying Nijinsky's photographs. He hoped that someday he would dance the roles Nijinsky had created.

On August 25, 1955, Rudolf Nureyev stood before the famous teacher Vera Kostravitskaya to be considered for a spot in the Leningrad Ballet School. The audition was a typical ballet class that was watched by a panel of experts. While a pianist played, the hopeful students were asked to perform exercises at the ballet barre, as well as jumps, turns, and other combinations in the center of the studio. The panelists evaluated the students not only for their talent, but also for their body proportions, musicality, and natural ability to move.

Kostravitskaya watched Rudolf with a severe and critical eye. She recognized his raw talent, but she had reservations. Perhaps she worried that at seventeen he was too old to begin serious ballet training — most students at the school had started at a much earlier age — or perhaps she sensed the rebelliousness that would chafe against the strict world of ballet. Whatever the case, at the end of the class, she predicted, "Young man, you'll either become a brilliant dancer — or a total failure!" She paused for a moment, then added forcefully, "And most likely you'll be a failure!"

In spite of her misgivings, Kostravitskaya recommended that he be allowed to join the school. For Rudolf, her assessment of his talent was simply another challenge to overcome. He was determined to prove her wrong. "From the moment of my acceptance, I decided not to allow anyone or anything to get in my way." His long-awaited dream had come true.

THE LENINGRAD BALLET SCHOOL

Intelligence and taste do not reside in the feet.
— Jean Georges Noverre (1727–1810)

At the age of seventeen, Rudolf Nureyev, the son of Tatar peasants, was officially accepted into the noble Leningrad Ballet School. His three years there would be marked by intensive ballet training, academics, his own self-development, and most dangerously, rebellion.

To appreciate why Rudolf was so determined to attend the Leningrad Ballet School, it is important to understand the unique role of the teacher in the art of ballet. It has been written, "Dancing is inspired by God. The science of dancing is taught by teachers." Maybe more than any other art form, dance requires its techniques, traditions, and choreography to be passed orally from one dancer or teacher down to the next generation. It is only recently that choreologists have developed universal and precise systems of "writing" dance movements, in much the same way as composers write music. In addition, we now have films and videos that capture the style and the choreography of a dance. But these modern advancements cannot breathe life into a movement — that inspiration must be passed on by a knowledgeable teacher.

Rudolf had dreamed of attending the Leningrad Ballet School

With Alla Sizova, posing for a picture for their graduation performance in June 1958.

41

because he knew that there he would be trained by the best teachers. In fact, when he enrolled, he was separated from the very beginnings of the art form by an unbroken line of only nine ballet masters (up both the French-Danish line and the Italian line of teachers). He was taught by instructors whose knowledge had been passed down over three hundred years by teachers who led directly back to ballet's first academy, the Académie Royale de Danse, which was established in 1661 by Louis XIV of France.

Ballet had its true origins in Italy during the Renaissance, when nobles staged extravagant pageants that included dance performances. But dance historians agree that the art form we know as ballet was born in the courts of the French kings. Catherine de Medici, who grew up in one of Italy's ruling families, introduced the Renaissance pageants into the French court in the middle of the sixteenth century, when she married the future king of France, Henri II. The spectacles her ballet masters staged were so successful that other European courts imitated them.

Very quickly, France established itself as the capital of ballet. Louis XIV, who himself enjoyed performing in the court ballets and was considered a fine dancer, founded his academy to train professional dancers and to lay the foundations of ballet. Initially, women participated only in the social dancing of the court; they did not perform before audiences until the 1680s. Instead, women's roles were played by male dancers. Over time, the French professionals, both men and women, developed new skills and introduced new steps, movements, and dances. Those trained professionals were in great demand at all the European courts, and so their innovations and knowledge spread. Even today, French is still the international language of ballet.

Like most ballet schools, the Leningrad school had its roots in France. In 1734, Empress Anna Ivanova invited a French ballet master, Jean Baptiste Landé, to come to Russia to instruct her *corps de cadets* (a group made up of young military men of noble birth). In those days, dance masters were employed by the rulers of Europe to teach their steps and routines not only to members of the court, but also to military officers. Dance training was used to improve an officer's speed, footwork, and mobility for fencing and hand-to-hand combat. Landé accepted the empress' invitation, and eventually sought permission to create a school of dance in St. Petersburg. "I humbly ask Your Majesty to order that I shall be given twelve Russian children — six males and six females — to create ballets and theater dances using twelve persons of comic and serious character," he wrote to her. "These pupils by the end of the first year will dance with cadets; in two years they will execute different dances; in three years they will not be less than the best foreign dancers." His request was granted in 1738, exactly two hundred years before Rudolf's birth. The school's first pupils were chosen from among the empress' servants.

Throughout the eighteenth century, ballet technique expanded, new staging concepts dramatically altered the way ballets were choreographed, and women continued to struggle to achieve equal status with men. Then, in the early nineteenth century, ballet entered its Romantic Age, and ballerinas began to dance on pointe, or on the tip of their toes. For the first time, female dancers became more prominent than males. For the most part, the new romantic ballets used the male dancers primarily to show off the grace of the ballerina.

There were still some key male figures in dance during the Romantic Age, however, and one of the most important was Marius Petipa, a dancer who arrived in St. Petersburg (the city was called Leningrad only from 1924 to 1991) in 1847. Petipa was appointed artistic director of the Imperial Ballet in 1862, and he served in that position under four tsars and for more than forty years. Although Russian rulers had always employed ballet masters of great distinction, such as Franz Hilverding and Charles

Didelot, it was Petipa who made Russia the world center of ballet.

Petipa is best known as a choreographer of more than sixty classical ballets, including *Swan Lake, Sleeping Beauty,* and *The Nutcracker.* He also established a distinctive Russian school of training that blended the refinement and grace of the French-Danish line with the dazzling technical virtuosity of the Italians. The Imperial School and its sister company produced many of ballet's legendary dancers: Anna Pavlova, Vaslav Nijinsky, Tamara Karsavina, and Michel Fokine.

Rudolf was poised to take his place among these great names of dance when he entered the Leningrad Ballet School in 1955. In fact, the routine he was expected to follow had changed little from the days when Nijinsky and Pavlova had studied there before the turn of the century.

The school was run with a profusion of rules and regulations, but Rudolf was not daunted. "I planned to feast on all the knowledge which ballet school had to offer." The daily schedule included eight to eleven hours of academic and dance studies, and Rudolf excelled in those subjects that most interested him — the histories of art, music, and dance. But his dance lessons brought him the most joy. Each day included a two-hour class in classical ballet technique, as well as additional classes in character dance (the techniques of national folk dances), pas de deux (dancing with a partner), or fencing (for the older male students).

The school's classes followed the Vaganova program, a method named for Agrippina Vaganova. She was a contemporary of Pavlova and Karsavina, and was considered a strong technician but not a beautiful dancer. Eventually, she came to be regarded as one of the twentieth century's greatest teachers. As Rudolf described the eight-year Vaganova training program, "It is a system in which a dancer is trained to move the entire body harmoniously as a single unit . . . not legs here and arms there, but in a way that body flows as one piece from dancer's feet to [his] head." When he entered the school, Rudolf was placed in the sixth level.

Rudolf relished the challenges the Leningrad Ballet School offered him, but, as he had in Ufa, he felt like an outcast. For one thing, his dormitory room housed twenty boys, and most were only fourteen or fifteen years old. At seventeen, he found the school's many rules too restrictive. "In my mind, rules were made more for younger students. I had journeyed too far a distance to be confined by what were unfair restrictions for someone of my age and experience."

Not surprisingly, it wasn't long before he had his first confrontation with the school's authorities. Soon after he arrived, he found out that a new epic ballet, *Taras Bulba,* was being performed at the Kirov Theater. Although students were absolutely forbidden to leave the residence at night without permission, Rudolf could not resist. He knew he could learn a great deal from watching the ballet, and rules weren't going to stand in his way. Without a word to anyone, he slipped out of the dormitory and made his way to the theater.

When his empty bed was discovered, the headmaster decided to teach the stubborn and rebellious Rudolf a lesson. He ordered his bed to be removed from the dormitory and took away the teenager's meal tickets. Rudolf returned from the theater to find that he had nowhere to sleep, and he spent the night huddled in a dark corner. Without meal tickets he could have no breakfast, so he went directly to his first class, where, exhausted and hungry, he promptly fainted.

The teacher sent him to Valentin Shelkov's office. Unfortunately for Rudolf, Shelkov was not only the director of the school, but also his sixth-form ballet teacher. Almost from the first day, their relationship had been strained. Shelkov often belittled Rudolf in class, calling him "a provincial good-for-nothing" and a "country boy," and constantly reminding him that he was at the school as a charity case. He drove Rudolf to tears nearly every day. This time, he berated him for breaking the rules.

At the Leningrad Ballet School: a defiant Rudolf; an unidentified former student; Alexander Pushkin; and Valentin Shelkov, Rudolf's adversary.

Rudolf realized that he would not survive at the school with Shelkov as his teacher. And if he was forced to leave, not only would his dream end, but he was old enough to be drafted into the army. So he mustered his courage and dared to ask Shelkov if he could be transferred. Caught off guard by Rudolf's impertinence, Shelkov agreed to send him to another teacher. Happily, the switch also elevated him to the eighth-year level. "It was act of self-preservation to request change of teachers," Rudolf explained years later. "Luckily, fate and good fortune took me by the hand and sent me to the class of Alexander Pushkin."

Alexander Pushkin was a highly respected teacher. Warm, generous, and sympathetic, he never raised his voice to his students. His pupils all remember him as a teacher who helped them master their technique without stifling their individual personalities. Rudolf always described Pushkin's class combinations as "dancy"; he never separated the steps from the music and from the dancer's emotions. Rudolf had bristled under the harsh, bullying ways first of his father and then of Shelkov.

*Rudolf with his teacher, mentor, and
"adopted" father, Alexander Pushkin.*

But Alexander Pushkin was a highly cultured man who both served as Rudolf's intellectual mentor and molded his rare talent. Under his caring and attentive guidance, the lonely teenager finally blossomed.

When Rudolf entered Pushkin's level-eight class, he was far behind the other students, most of whom had been steeped in the school's strict ballet program for years. Rudolf's training had been much less intensive and coordinated. One day, several classmates gathered around and shoved him in front of the studio mirrors. "Look at yourself, Nureyev," they declared. "You'll never be able to dance — it just isn't possible. You're simply not built for it. You have nothing — no schooling and no technique. How do you have the nerve to work with us?"

Rudolf was stung by their words. He knew that what they said about his lack of technique was true. But he also knew that technique could be improved, and that all he needed was some time to catch up. He stood in front of the mirror and stared at his reflection. Although he was often frustrated with his body, he did not agree with his fellow students' claim

"When I came to study in Leningrad, I always wanted to know why you should do this or that as much as how you made it happen."

that he was not built for dancing. Maybe his body wasn't perfect, but how many bodies were? "No," he thought, "I'll prove them wrong."

Prove them wrong he did, for although Rudolf had some shortcomings, he was also blessed with many strengths. Despite all his rebelliousness, he took corrections and applied them immediately. He could learn steps in a fraction of the time it took anyone else. And he possessed near-superhuman levels of energy and stamina. Long after his classmates had left the studio, he continued to work by himself. Standing in front of the mirror, hour after hour and day after day, he worked not only on his line, his jumps, and his turns, but also on the movements that connected the steps. He tried to perfect each hand gesture and every tilt of the head. He was rarely satisfied with himself.

As time passed, Rudolf caught up with the others in the class, but he remained a loner. According to his fellow students, he could be rude, defiant, and bad-tempered. In all likelihood, he inherited his fiery temper from his father, but Rudolf enjoyed giving the credit to his fierce Tatar ancestry. "Tatars are quick to catch fire," he liked to say. "Our Tatar blood runs faster. It is always at boiling point." But it wasn't just his gruff manner and his quickness to anger that got him labeled a troublemaker. He was also viewed suspiciously because he showed so little interest in the school's Communist youth organization – the Komsomol. Everyone in the Soviet Union was expected to be a loyal follower of Communist doctrine, and it was widely understood that Rudolf's lack of interest could hinder his future career. Fearing that associating with him could paint them as rebels, many of the other students kept their distance.

The few friends Rudolf did make – Sergiu Stefanschi from Romania, Menia Martinez from Cuba, and Leo Ahonen from Finland – were usually foreigners, and hence outsiders like him. Stefanschi's bed was next to Rudolf's in the dormitory. Even though Stefanschi was three years younger, Rudolf constantly asked him what he was learning in his classes;

Leningrad's Palace Square. At its center is the Alexander Column, around which Rudolf and his friends chased each other in circles of grand jetés.

he would use Stefanschi's classroom corrections to improve his own technique. Stefanschi remembers, "Rudolf never stopped trying to improve himself, even up until the lights were turned out."

On the few occasions when the students were allowed to attend the theater, Rudolf, Ahonen, and Stefanschi often found themselves so inspired that they could not sleep. Recalling those nights, Stefanschi told me, "We would creep into a hallway and stay up all night repeating the steps we had seen. We would take turns doing the male and female roles so that we could practice our partnering. Occasionally, one of us would wickedly mimic one of the performers, and this merrymaking brought on gales of laughter. For fear of being caught, we jumped all over each other trying to stifle one another's laughter."

When they were a little older, the three young men were moved to the ground floor of the dormitory. During the so-called White Nights of Leningrad, the time of year when the summer sun sets over that northern city for only a few hours after midnight and even normal people seem to have extra energy, the boys could not stand being locked inside. As often as they could, they climbed out the window into the endless twilight and headed for the Palace Square in front of the Hermitage Museum. In the center of the square stands the largest granite column in the world – the Alexander Column, erected in 1834 to honor Tsar Alexander I's victory over Napoleon. Around the mighty structure, the three teenagers chased each other in a circle of grand jetés, each competing to jump faster, farther, or higher than the other. By some miracle, their antics were never reported to the school.

Although Rudolf was finally beginning to make some friends and enjoy himself, he was still focused primarily on improving his dancing. As he matured, he began to realize that becoming an artist would require more of him than raw talent and hard work. Years later, he would quote the eighteenth-century ballet master Jean Georges Noverre, who said, "It is imperative for dancers to divide their time and studies between the mind and the body. . . . Intelligence and taste do not reside in the feet."

Fortunately, Rudolf was insatiably curious. During his free time, he set himself on a demanding course of self-improvement, visiting museums and attending concerts and the theater. Remarkably, this loner became a magnet for people of all ages, most of whom were eager to help him satisfy his interests. One of his favorite discoveries was a special music shop, where he became friendly with the assistant, Elisaveta Pazhi. She introduced Rudolf to music that was new to him and even found him a piano teacher, Marina Petrovna Savva, who gave him free lessons.

Through Pazhi and Savva, Rudolf met the Romankovs and their children, Liuba and her twin brother, Leonid. Both were physics students at the Leningrad Polytechnic Institute. The Romankovs immediately accepted Rudolf into their home, and this brought balance to his cloistered ballet-school life. In Liuba and Leonid, he found friends his own age in whom he could confide, and it was with their tutor that he secretly began learning English. (The desire to learn English, and indeed any other Western language, was viewed with suspicion by the Soviet authorities because it was considered evidence of too great an interest in communicating with "undesirable" foreigners.)

At the end of his first year, Rudolf convinced Alexander Pushkin to allow him to perform the male solo from the technically difficult "Diana and Acteon" pas de deux for the school's year-end examination. Pushkin felt that Rudolf was not yet ready to do the exam, but he let him try. His performance astonished everyone, and finally brought the school troublemaker a measure of respect and acceptance from teachers and students alike. From that point on, life became a little easier for him.

Normally Rudolf would have had to complete only one more year, but owing to his late start he was advised by Pushkin to take two more polishing years at the school. As he neared the end of his final term, he was invited to compete in the inaugural Moscow Ballet Competition. He chose his parts carefully to show off "not only my strong technique, but roles which demonstrated a range of styles and emotions." He was to dance with a fellow student, Alla Sizova.

Those who witnessed the competition still remember how passionately Rudolf danced. One spectator raved, "He was explosive! No one made a bigger impression." During one of the evening shows, the audience stamped and applauded for an encore. After that performance, fellow students crowded around him with congratulations. Vladimir Vasiliev, the Bolshoi Ballet's best young dancer and a future superstar, was especially impressed. He exclaimed, "You have dazzled and captivated us, Rudolf!"

Tantalizing offers of solo contracts came to Rudolf from both the

Bolshoi and the Stanislavsky companies, two of the best in the USSR. But before he could even consider these offers, he had to return to Leningrad to perform his graduation examination.

Once again, he triumphed. After his performance, Natalia Dudinskaya, the Kirov's prima ballerina, searched for him backstage. "Rudolf," she urged, "don't be foolish. Don't choose the Bolshoi. Stay here and we'll dance together." He was only twenty years old, and one of the world's most admired ballerinas was asking him to dance with her.

After only three years at the Leningrad Ballet School, Rudolf had completed the entire Vaganova training program and was accepted into the Kirov Ballet — not as a member of the corps de ballet, but as a soloist. In the entire history of the great company, only two other men had earned such an honor — Michel Fokine and Vaslav Nijinsky.

4

THE KIROV BALLET

He came . . . and he conquered.
— Vera Krasovskaya, a famous Russian dance critic

As a young boy in the Ufa Opera House, crushed in a crowded box seat between his sisters, Rudolf had promised himself that he would become a dancer. Now the rehearsal was over, and his real life was about to begin. Rudolf was at last a member of the great Kirov Ballet.

Nothing in Rudolf's career had happened according to the rules, and his entry into the Kirov was no exception. Almost all young dancers initially join a classical company as a member of the corps de ballet. It is in the corps that they become accustomed to performing and, over time, hone their technique and stagecraft. Also, most companies already have many experienced soloists and principal dancers waiting to be cast in a limited number of leading roles — the Kirov, for instance, had stars who gave only ten or fifteen performances a year — so a new dancer would have few chances to perform if he or she was assigned only featured parts.

Astonishingly, Rudolf never danced in the corps de ballet. Almost immediately after joining the Kirov, he began to prepare for his first principal role: he would dance the part of Frondoso in *Laurencia*. In this Spanish-inspired story, Frondoso and his fiancée, Laurencia, lead their

Rudolf as Frondoso in Laurencia, *his first starring role, with the Kirov's prima ballerina, Natalia Dudinskaya.*

village in a rebellion against a cruel overlord. As Rudolf was promised, his partner would be the forty-six-year-old prima ballerina Natalia Dudinskaya, for whom the role of Laurencia had been created by Vakhtang Chaboukiani in 1939.

Rudolf debuted in his first starring role on November 20, 1958. According to Ninel Kurgapkina, another revered Kirov ballerina, he showed himself to be a confident partner, a skilled technician, and a gifted performer — attributes that many ballet dancers need years to acquire. When the lights came up after the performance, the audience exploded in thunderous applause. During the curtain calls, whispers rippled through the theater on both sides of the footlights: "He is the next one!" and "A new star is born!"

Looking back on the fantastic night, Rudolf would later say, "As an inexperienced young dancer, it was a tremendous challenge to dance this ballet with Dudinskaya. She instilled in me a strong sense of classicism, attack, and musicality, and an image of how to spin in turns. Still in my dancing today, I call on those lessons. I will remain forever grateful to her."

Over time, as one superb performance followed another, the public became obsessed with the Kirov's new star. Sergiu Stefanschi recalls, "A cult of fans developed around Rudolf — they were *absolute* fanatics. They showered him with flowers from the balconies in the middle of the performance. Of course, the performance had to be stopped while the stage was cleared of the flowers. So a ban was put into place against anyone bringing flowers into the theater on Rudolf's performance days. That did not stop his fans. It may seem unbelievable, but there were women who hid their bouquets underneath their dresses before they entered the theater."

Of course, it wasn't all curtain calls and applause and bouquets. Rudolf had not been with the Kirov long when he took on his familiar role of rebel. It was not that he deliberately set out to break the rules; he simply paid no attention to them. His loyalty was only to his own talent. Yet acts of defiance were rare in the tradition-bound world of professional ballet, and rarer still in Russian society of the time. Rudolf's attitude, combined with his jealousy-provoking talent, won him few friends among the members of the company. He didn't seem to mind, however. He did not seek or need the approval of his peers. He cared only about dancing.

Despite being an inexperienced newcomer, Rudolf charged through the Kirov's rules and traditions like a bull in a china shop when he thought they stood in the way of him dancing his best. He caused a great stir, for instance, when he insisted on changes to his costumes. At the time, Russian male dancers wore long tunics and short bloomers over their tights for modesty. In an effort to make his legs look longer, Rudolf shortened the tunics and refused to put on the trunks. "Why should I wear these lampshades?" he protested. "In the West, they've been dancing in tights for years, and so will I!"

Rudolf's acts of rebellion did not stop with his costumes; he also made refinements to the standard way individual steps were performed. To make his arms and legs look longer, he created techniques that gave him the pleasing lines more often associated with female dancers. He even borrowed features he thought would improve his dancing from male dancers in the West (he'd seen images of some in dance magazines and films that had been smuggled into Russia). For example, when Russian male dancers rose on their toes, they traditionally rose only to quarter-pointe, with their heels just slightly off the ground. Rudolf was the first Russian male dancer to dance high up on his toes on demi-pointe, another innovation meant to make his legs appear longer. As well, he was the first Russian male dancer to execute pirouettes with his foot above the base of his knee in high passé. He also exaggerated the crossing of his feet in fifth position and worked to lift his legs as high as possible.

Not content with revising his costumes and his technique, Rudolf went on to create an uproar when he dared to alter the choreography of some

In rehearsal at the Kirov.

of the Kirov's most well-known ballets. In *La Bayadère*, an exotic story about Solor, a noble Indian warrior who is loved by two women, Rudolf changed one of his solos to include a circle of double assemblé turns, a series of fiendishly difficult spins in the air. At the time, his change was considered to be astonishingly impertinent. Today, it has become the standard.

That Rudolf was allowed to break with tradition and make his individual mark is a testament to the Kirov management's high regard for his talent. Normally, any ballet company in the world would have punished a dancer as obstinate and difficult as Rudolf. Indeed, in 1911, when the legendary Vaslav Nijinsky refused to wear his shorts in *Giselle*, the Maryinsky Ballet immediately dismissed him from the company.

Late in Rudolf's first Kirov season, he was scheduled to dance *Laurencia* again. On the afternoon before the performance, he spent hours practicing alone in front of the studio mirror. Over and over, he forced himself to repeat each turn and leap. That evening, a ballet master, perhaps unaware of the work Rudolf had already done that day, insisted that the exhausted dancer continue rehearsing. Disaster struck. Rudolf tore a ligament in his right leg. When a doctor predicted that he would not dance for two years, he was overcome with despair.

Alexander Pushkin rushed to the hospital, where he found Rudolf deeply depressed. The teacher was more worried about his pupil's mental state than he was about the injury, and he made plans to move the young man into his own two-room apartment. There, he and his wife, Xenia, a former dancer herself, cared for Rudolf as tenderly as if he were their own son. In this warm and loving environment, Rudolf's despair began to lift, and he recovered in record time. In only three weeks, he was back at rehearsals.

The Pushkins' tight living arrangements were typical for the Russia of the 1950s. Housing was still in short supply after the war, which had left an estimated twenty-five million people homeless, and even rising stars like Rudolf lived in difficult surroundings. "When I left school, I was assigned one room with eight other people," he remembered. "We slept on beds nailed to wall like shelves, one on top of other." Rudolf, of course, had known terrible living conditions as a child. But even he would cringe when describing those claustrophobic quarters and his motley crew of roommates, who were often from walks of life far removed from the dance world.

Not long after his successful debut, he was assigned an apartment that was luxurious by Russian standards of the time. But he never lived in it, preferring to stay with the Pushkins even after he'd recovered from his injury. Both Pushkins looked after his artistic needs, and Xenia also took care of Rudolf's meals and laundry. The Pushkins were his adopted family now.

Though he was beginning to make a home for himself offstage, and had certainly made his mark onstage, the hot-tempered Rudolf contin- ued to make enemies in the wings. Many Kirov members felt it was unfair that he was allowed to get away with so much, and they deeply resented the preferential treatment he received. As a result, his deepest friendships were formed with people outside the company. Tamara Zakrzhevskaya, a university student, was one. She remembers Rudolf as "forever on the look-out for something new to fill in the gaps of his education. He often asked me, 'What did you learn at university today?'" To aid him in his quest for knowledge, Tamara obtained permission for Rudolf to attend some of her university lectures, and together they haunted museums and attended countless concerts and ballets.

Rudolf's thirst for knowledge knew no bounds. Since the days he had spent watching the trains leave the station in Ufa, he had dreamed of traveling the world. He wanted to see other countries with his own eyes, and he especially wanted to see their dancers and ballet companies. But

This picture was taken by Rudolf's friend Tamara Zakrzhevskaya as he prepared to go on tour with the Kirov Ballet.

travel to the West was a rare privilege in Communist Russia, and only people who were trusted — usually loyal Communist Party members — were allowed to leave. In 1959, the Kirov selected a group of young dancers to perform at the World Youth Festival in Vienna, Austria. Rudolf, to no one's surprise, was not included. Who knew how the volatile dancer would behave in the West? His rebelliousness and his disdain for politics had finally come back to haunt him.

The distraught Rudolf pleaded with the company's director to give him the opportunity to dance in Vienna. Although the director had serious misgivings, he also had no doubt that Rudolf's talent would add to the company's stellar reputation. He reluctantly added the renegade dancer to the group, but his misgivings proved to be well-founded. The trip marked the beginning of a series of much more dangerous clashes between Rudolf and the Soviet authorities.

In Vienna, everything went well. Rudolf and his partner, Alla Sizova, placed first among several gold-prize winners. But on the journey home, when the group had to change trains in Kiev, Rudolf took off in a cab to see the ancient city. Unluckily, his taxi got caught in a traffic jam, and he missed the train. The other dancers were so sure that the incident would end his career at the Kirov that they immediately started guessing how his roles would be divided among them.

Missing a train, missing a political meeting, showing a bent for independence — small acts, each one, but the stakes were high for ignoring the rules. In the past, other dancers had been exiled to ballet companies in Siberia, and sometimes more than a person's career was on the line. Defying the government could mean prison or even death.

During Rudolf's years at the Kirov, he was often attacked for not conforming to the ways of the Communist regime. If he was seen spending too much time with any foreign dancers who happened to be visiting or studying in Leningrad, he was called into the director's office and warned to cut off his friendships. When the American cast of *My Fair Lady* came to the city, Rudolf rushed anxiously to see the production. The Russian secret police, the KGB, watched as he mingled with the performers after the show. Again, he faced an interrogation for his "outrageous" conduct. He was never able to understand why he was criticized simply for being curious.

Time and time again, Rudolf was saved by the sheer uniqueness of his talent. The Russian critics called him "a virtuoso" and "a leading dancer in the heroic mold." After his first performance of *Giselle*, with Irina Kolpakova, the famous Russian critic Vera Krasovskaya wrote, "There is little doubt that few believed wholeheartedly in the success of the fiery Nureyev as Albrecht. But he came . . . and he conquered."

Giselle, one of ballet's most famous and romantic stories, was first performed in Paris in 1841. In it, a sweet village girl, Giselle, falls in love with Albrecht, a stranger whom she believes is a fellow peasant. By the end of the first act, Albrecht is revealed to be a count who must marry a duchess. Shocked by Albrecht's betrayal, Giselle loses her mind and dies of a broken heart. In the eerie forest scene of act 2, the grieving Albrecht visits Giselle's moonlit grave. He is confronted by the ghostly Wilis — jilted maidens who after death are condemned to wander restlessly through the forest and dance through the night. For his cruelty to Giselle, Albrecht is condemned by the Queen of the Wilis to dance until he dies. Rising from the dead, Giselle protects Albrecht until the dawn, when the Wilis must all return to their graves.

Giselle was such a well-known and beloved ballet that to suggest any changes to it was considered scandalous. Yet once again, Rudolf challenged tradition, altering his costume and modifying a famous dance sequence in act 2. Even more shockingly, he changed the very character of Albrecht. Instead of making him a noble cad who later feels regret for having broken a maiden's heart, Rudolf depicted him as a tragic, romantic, and much more human figure from the beginning. He made the audience care desperately for a man who was torn between love and his royal obligations. One of Russia's leading critics wrote, in a review for the American *Atlantic Monthly*, "On December 14, 1959, the inhabitants of Leningrad literally besieged the Kirov Theater trying to attend the performance of the well-known ballet *Giselle*, though the performers were only beginners. The part of Albrecht was danced by the Bashkir, Rudolf Nureyev. Nureyev has an extraordinary natural talent. . . . His Albrecht is unlike anyone's we have ever seen."

Rudolf's mother, Farida, was in the audience for his debut in *Giselle*. It was the first time she had seen her son dance on the Kirov stage. The response of the audience astonished her, and Rudolf's moving performance made her cry. The following spring, both of his parents came to Leningrad to watch him perform. His father had never seen his son dance before any audience. Rudolf told me that Hamet was surprised by the audience's near-hysterical reaction to his son's performance. "For first time he was proud of me, and finally he understood my need to dance."

In the autumn of 1960, American Ballet Theatre toured the Soviet Union, marking the first time an American dance troupe had been permitted to visit. Rudolf was desperately disappointed to learn that he would not be able to see the group perform. He was being sent on a bus tour to dance in East Germany while the Americans were in Leningrad.

Rudolf later described that tour as ghastly. "I was perpetually cold and tired, and my legs were in a dreadfully bad condition. Once we had to wait for eight hours on an icy bus . . . for it to be repaired. On other occasions we would arrive at six o'clock and by half past six we would be dancing at a café before an indifferent, half-drunk audience." He also knew that he was missing the opportunity to see not only the American company, but also its guest artist, Erik Bruhn, the great Danish dancer who was known for his flawless technique and fascinating interpretations of roles.

The temporary exile made Rudolf furious. As soon as he returned from the East German tour, he stormed into the director's office to complain bitterly. The director repaid the dancer's insolence by sending him on yet another tortuous tour — this time to northern Russia with a circus company. In December!

Rudolf danced one performance in the frigid Arctic cold and flatly refused to continue the tour. Instead, he caught the first train to Moscow.

When he arrived, he was ordered to appear at the ministry of culture. There, he was informed that he would be punished in two ways. First, he would never be allowed to dance before any high-ranking government official (this was a hollow threat to a person who had so little respect for authority). Second — and much more disastrously — he would never again be allowed to leave Russia.

After years of being unconcerned about rules, Rudolf was finally frightened. He knew that his company was making plans for its first appearance in the West — a tour to Paris and London. Given the ban on his travel, he held out little hope that he would be included. But he decided that he would try everything in his power to convince officials to change their minds. He would work hard, make no trouble, and try to control his now-famous temper.

This period was productive. Rudolf performed many of the leading roles in the Kirov's major ballets, and he partnered several of the company's foremost ballerinas, including Ninel Kurgapkina, Irina Kolpakova, Alla Sizova, Alla Osipenko, and Alla Shelest, whom he later described as his favorite. He also debuted as the Prince in both *Swan Lake* and *Sleeping Beauty.*

Then fate turned in his favor. Natalia Dudinskaya's husband, Konstantin Sergeyev, was the Kirov's newly appointed director and its leading male dancer. When the tour organizers in Paris let it be known that the fifty-year-old Sergeyev was considered too old to perform for the supercritical French audiences, he replaced himself with the talented but troublesome Nureyev.

On the day of departure, Rudolf said his good-byes to Tamara, Liuba, Leonid, Rosa, and of course, his beloved Pushkins. Although none of them knew it then, years would pass before he next saw Rosa and his friends. He was never to see Alexander or Xenia Pushkin again.

May 11, 1961. Paris at last! Rehearsals at the opera house consumed the

Konstantin Sergeyev and Alexander Pushkin preparing Rudolf for the Kirov's first tour to the West.

days, but Rudolf's hunger to experience Paris drew him out on the streets every night. He loved the city and its atmosphere. When he befriended some dancers from the Paris Opéra, they happily showed off their hometown to the eager Rudolf. But while he and the French dancers — who included Claire Motte, Pierre Lacotte, and Jean-Pierre Bonnefous — were freely roaming the city, the other Kirov dancers were obediently sightseeing on the company's organized bus tour. Rudolf's blatant disobedience once again attracted the attention of the company's authorities, who warned him that his behavior was unacceptable. The KGB agents who had been sent by the government to guard the dancers also took notice.

Sergeyev did not schedule Rudolf to dance in the Kirov's opening-night performance of *Sleeping Beauty* on May 16. However, he did have him perform in the general dress rehearsal before an invited audience of journalists, influential French citizens, and ballet enthusiasts. Rudolf's rehearsal appearance caused a sensation, and news of the Kirov's extraordinary young dancer spread quickly. It was not until May 19, however, that the Parisian public was at last treated to Rudolf's first performance. He danced one of his favorite parts, the role of the warrior Solor in *La Bayadère*, and by the time the curtain fell, he had conquered Paris. The audience went mad.

In the days that followed, critics lavished praise on Rudolf. "The Kirov Has Found Its Cosmonaut, Rudolf Nureyev!" and "The Leningrad Ballet Has Its Own Man in Space," ran the headlines. Another writer called him a Sputnik rocket. (The references to space travel suggested not only Rudolf's soaring leaps, but also the space race that was taking place between the Soviet Union and the United States. It was a high-stakes competition to see which country would be first to launch a man into orbit. Only one month before Rudolf's first performance in the West, the Soviets had won that race. On April 12, 1961, Yuri Gagarin, a Russian cosmonaut, became the first man to orbit the earth.)

Although Rudolf was under KGB orders to stay away from foreigners, he went out to celebrate with his new Western friends after his first triumphant performance. That evening, he met Clara Saint, a beautiful girl who was engaged to the son of France's minister of culture. Throughout Rudolf's stay in Paris, he and Saint spent much time together, becoming close friends.

For the KGB, his refusal to stay away from the Westerners was the last straw. This was as far as this young dancer would push them! From the night of his first performance, they never left Rudolf alone. Two agents were posted outside the doors of his hotel room and his dressing room at all times. They did not care that Rudolf was the toast of Paris. As far as they were concerned, he was out of control and had to be punished. The decision was made to send him back to Russia immediately.

Sergeyev pleaded Rudolf's case. He insisted that the dancer be allowed to remain with the Kirov for the company's month-long stay in France. The young star was creating a sensation in Paris, Sergeyev pointed out, so if they sent him home in the middle of the tour, embarrassing questions would be asked by the press.

These perilous, behind-the-scenes negotiations took place without Rudolf's knowledge, so he was unaware of the immediate danger he was creating by ignoring Sergeyev's repeated warnings to stop associating with "undesirables." Instead, he took the warnings as yet another attempt to stifle his curiosity. He was aware, however, of what had become the constant, shadowy presence of the KGB agents.

Soon, the month-long reprieve Sergeyev had won for him was up. On Rudolf's last evening in Paris, he and Saint strolled along the streets, savoring the late spring air. He would miss the beautiful city, but he was excited about dancing in London. Reluctantly, he returned to his hotel; there was barely enough time to pack his things.

The moment he opened his suitcase, he realized that someone had gone through his belongings. His roommate, Yuri Soloviev, admitted that the KGB had forced him to search Rudolf's bag. It was a difficult moment between them, but ultimately Rudolf did not blame Soloviev. He understood that for most people it was normal to obey the authorities. Still, the incident was unsettling.

When the company arrived at Le Bourget Airport, a throng of French ballet enthusiasts had gathered to say good-bye to the dancers. Rudolf spotted some of his new French friends in the waiting area and joined them for a final drink at the bar. Sergeyev found him there and drew him aside. "Rudi," he said, "you won't be coming with us now. You'll join us in London in a couple of days. We've just received a wire from Moscow saying that you are to dance in the Kremlin tomorrow. So we'll be leaving you now, and you'll take the Tupolev [a Russian plane], which leaves in two hours' time."

Rudolf felt sick with fear. His face turned ashen and his eyes welled up. He knew that Sergeyev was lying about appearing at the Kremlin.

FREEDOM DASH BY RED DANCER

From PETER STEPHENS, Paris, Friday

RUSSIAN ballet star Rudolf Noureev today asked for political asylum in France after a dramatic scene in which Soviet agents tried to kidnap him at Le Bourget Airport.

Noureev, 22, was about to board a plane for London with the rest of the famous Leningrad State Kirov Ballet troupe when Russian officials approached him.

Scream

After a few words they tried to hustle him on to a Moscow-bound jet airliner.

Suddenly Noureev screamed: "I want to stay free! I want to stay free!"—and began struggling with the Russians while passengers looked on.

In a running fight across the airport hall, Noureev tore himself away from the Russian agents as French airport police dashed up.

Scuffle

There was a sharp scuffle between the plain-clothes Russians and the French police before Noureev was escorted to safety in the police office.

Later, French officials said he had asked for political asylum, and his request would be granted.

Both the Russian jet and the ballet troupe's chartered British Vanguard left the airport forty-five minutes late.

With Noureev today was twenty-one-year-old Clara Saint, attractive daughter of a Chilean industrialist, who lives in Paris.

"We are very good friends," she told me last night. "I watched Rudolf dance nearly every night during the three weeks he was in Paris, and met him after each performance.

"But there was nothing serious between us. I have no idea why he asked for asylum. We never discussed politics."

Other friends of the dancer said Noureev had behaved "very independently" in Paris, and had been allowed considerable freedom.

IN LONDON when the Kirov troupe arrived last night, officials could not agree on an explanation of Noureev's absence.

Said administrator Mr. Valentin Bogdanov: "Our numbers are all correct. There is no one missing."

Returned

Another official, Mr. F. Feodorov, said: "Noureev has returned to Leningrad because his mother is dying."

And a red-jacketed Russian woman interpreter said: "Noureev was called back to Moscow for another performance."

The Kirov troupe are due to start a four-week season at the Royal Opera House, Covent Garden, on Monday.

The headline from London's Daily Mirror, *Saturday, June 17, 1961.*

Hadn't the authorities warned him that he would never dance before high-ranking officials again? He also knew that punishment awaited him back in Russia. He would be exiled to Siberia or even imprisoned. He would certainly never be allowed to return to the West again.

As soon as Sergeyev left, Rudolf turned to one his friends, Pierre Lacotte. "I am finished," he pleaded. "Help me." Lacotte asked Jean-Pierre Bonnefous to call Clara Saint and tell her to come immediately to the airport. Perhaps, with her connections to France's minister of culture, she could help.

While all this was going on, the Russian dancers were gathering up their belongings and getting ready for their flight. Rudolf approached them with tears in his eyes. All the old rivalries were forgotten in the urgency of the moment. The dancers were frightened for him, for they knew what the order meant. Some of the ballerinas began to cry, begging, "Stay calm, Rudolf, and don't make a fuss. Return to Moscow quietly."

Rudolf watched the rest of the company board the plane to London, then glanced anxiously around the waiting room. Some KGB agents had been left to guard him and, if necessary, physically put him on the plane to Russia. But he knew that if he got on that plane, his career — and perhaps his life — was over.

Suddenly, Clara Saint rushed through the door. Bonnefous led her to Rudolf, who was flanked by two threatening guards. As she leaned in to give Rudolf a kiss, he whispered urgently in English, a language the agents did not understand, "Do something." Immediately, she went in search of the airport police.

The two tall KGB agents continued to keep watch on either side of him. When Saint finally returned, Rudolf was upset to see that she was alone. Once again, she leaned in to offer Rudolf a final farewell kiss, then quickly whispered that two airport police officers would casually appear and stand a few yards away from him. It was up to him to approach them. By law, they could not influence a foreign citizen to defect.

Minutes later, the gendarmes came into view. Rudolf's heart pounded. He was drenched in nervous perspiration. He wanted to run immediately to them, but he waited and calculated. Then, almost imperceptibly, he felt his guards relax their vigilance. Seizing the moment, he flew towards the French officers. Throwing himself into their arms, he cried, "I want to stay! I want to be free!" The KGB agents lunged after him, grabbing at his limbs. A terrible tug-of-war ensued, but it lasted for only a few moments. The gendarmes were firm with the Russians: "Messieurs!" they declared. "This is France." Reluctantly, the agents let Rudolf go.

The next day, newspapers all over the world heralded, "Russian Dancer Leaps to Freedom!"

5

FREEDOM

Then and there, I decided never to look back.
— Rudolf Nureyev

Rudolf had known so much suppression in his life: the stifling, crowded rooms of his childhood; his father's disapproval; his family's poverty; and hanging over everything, an authoritarian political regime. At last, he was free — to dance what he wanted and where he wanted, to say what he felt, to choose his friends, to travel, to follow his curiosity wherever it took him. He was truly free.

It had all happened so fast. Once the KGB agents had let him go, the gendarmes led the distraught dancer away to the safety of their offices. Rudolf was told he would have to sign a request for an official sanctuary permit, but first he was taken into a small, private room to think over his decision. A French official showed him that the room had two doors. One door led into the main hall; if he changed his mind about his defection, he could walk through it and board the plane back to the Soviet Union. The other door led into the office of the French police; if he chose that door, he would be allowed to stay in France. They left him alone in the small room to make the most difficult decision of his life.

Discussing his first appearance in London with Dame Margot Fonteyn. "Almost every-thing I learned about handling career in West, I learned from Margot," he once said.

Isolated and in silence, Rudolf tried to make sense of his chaotic thoughts. He reflected on the many obstacles he had overcome to make it to the Kirov School, and on how hard he'd worked to be accepted into the company. Now he would never be allowed to dance with them again. He worried about his friends, his family, and the Pushkins. Would they understand his actions? He knew his decision to stay in the West would break their hearts. Would any of them be punished because of him? Would he ever see them again?

Although all these thoughts swirled about in his mind, Rudolf knew that there was no real choice for him. If he returned to the Soviet Union, he faced the fury of the KGB. There was the very real possibility of exile to Siberia or, worse, execution. At the very least, he concluded, they would never allow him to dance again, and Rudolf knew that would make his life unbearable. There was only one choice he could make. He got up from his chair and opened the door that led to the office of the French police — and to freedom.

Rudolf's defection on June 16, 1961, took place at the height of the Cold War. It was a time of fearful tension and powerful competition between the Communist countries of the Soviet Empire and the democracies of the West. In that uneasy international atmosphere, the press turned Rudolf into a symbol for all people who sought freedom. His "leap to freedom," as it was called in the media, caught the imagination of people all over the world. At the age of twenty-three, he had become a hero in the West and an embarrassing traitor in the USSR.

For Rudolf, who had been born on a train racing across Asia, life began again in an airport in the West. Like a newborn, he had no clothes and no possessions (they were on their way to London with the Kirov Ballet). All he had was what he carried within him: his intelligence, an iron will, a strong sense of self-reliance, and his talent. But adjusting to a new way of life in the West would not be easy. He had to deal with his sadness and a gnawing worry for the loved ones he'd left behind. And there was the very real threat of being injured, kidnapped, or even killed by the KGB. From that first week, threats against his safety became a fact of Rudolf's life. He was followed by the same agents who had held him at the airport, and he was hounded by anonymous death threats. (Nearly one year after his defection, Rudolf was tried by the Russian government in his absence. He was charged with treason, a crime that was punishable by death by firing squad. Found guilty, he was given a seven-year prison sentence and remained on the KGB's "most wanted" list for decades.)

Rudolf was also concerned about how he was going to make a living, but that problem was solved within a few days when the Marquis de Cuevas Ballet Company offered him a generous contract. Rudolf was relieved, but he would commit to the troupe for only a short term because he had other dreams, including dancing with George Balanchine's company in New York City. He also wanted to go to Denmark to study with the ballet masters who had taught his idol, Erik Bruhn. Rudolf considered Bruhn to be the best male dancer in the world.

On June 23, just one week after his defection, Rudolf performed with his first Western company. He danced the role of the Prince in the Marquis de Cuevas production of *Sleeping Beauty* before an audience overflowing with supporters. They welcomed him to the West with a standing ovation and twenty-eight curtain calls.

But not every performance went that well. On a subsequent evening, a photographer came backstage just before the curtain went up and handed Rudolf three envelopes. One was from his mother, one from his father, and one from Alexander Pushkin. Something told him he shouldn't read the letters before he danced, just in case the messages upset him. But he tore open the envelopes anyway, longing for some reassuring words from those who loved him.

He should have trusted his instincts. Each of the letters begged him to come home and not to squander his life in the West. "Don't be a traitor to your country," read the one from his father. He was emotionally shattered. It was only later, when he had more time to think about why those letters had been written, that he realized the KGB was trying to destroy him through the people he loved. Agents had forced his parents and Pushkin to write the letters.

That same evening, when he began to dance the Bluebird pas de deux in the third act of *Sleeping Beauty*, real pandemonium broke out. Rudolf and his partner, Beatrice Consuelo, had barely stepped on the stage when a near riot erupted in the audience. Loud screaming, piercing whistles, thunderous stomping of feet came from people trying to disrupt the orchestra and stop the performance. They shouted "Traitor!" and "Go back to Moscow!" Broken glass was thrown from the balconies, and paper bombs filled with pepper were hurled at the stage. The KGB had planted French-Communist agitators in the theater to terrorize Rudolf and the ballet company that had hired him.

But neither the musicians nor the dancers faltered. Even though it was almost impossible to hear the music, the performance continued. Finally, the police arrived and, with the help of members of the audience, removed those causing the commotion. When the evening was over, Rudolf was more certain than ever that his decision to defect had been the correct one. "I survived that awful night, and it gave me new strength. Then and there I decided never to look back. I would live my life for present and for future."

All his life, Rudolf had made his own opportunities. But there had also been people in Russia – his early ballet teachers, Natalia Dudinskaya, the Pushkins, and his friends in Leningrad – who had helped him achieve his goals. When he arrived in the West, he expected to have to push

Erik Bruhn coaching Rudolf in 1965. "I wanted to learn everything I could from Erik. To me, he was the best dancer in the world."

forward alone. To his surprise, however, some of the most talented people in ballet in Paris, Copenhagen, and London lent him a helping hand and made some remarkable opportunities for him.

Following the de Cuevas Ballet's Paris season, Rudolf left for Copenhagen to take classes with Erik Bruhn's Danish teachers (the artistic descendants of the teacher-choreographer August Bournonville) and the famous Russian teacher Vera Volkova. As children, Volkova and

Alexander Pushkin had studied together under the renowned dancer Nicolas Legat. Another of her teachers had been Agrippina Vaganova.

While studying with the Royal Danish Ballet, Rudolf finally met Erik Bruhn. Ever since he had missed seeing Bruhn dance in Russia, he dreamed of meeting him and learning all he could from the dancer. When he told me about that first meeting with his idol, he observed, "You know how it is when you first meet someone you admire. . . . There is fear of being disappointed. Sometimes, your idol does not live up to your expectations. But with Erik, I was enormously impressed. From beginning, we had instant meeting of minds and hearts." The thirty-three-year-old Dane was a dancer of perfect proportions and immaculate technique, and he had the picture-perfect face of a prince. In Bruhn, Rudolf had found not only another artist with whom he could share his devotion to their craft, but also a mentor, a confidant, and a friend.

Bruhn was equally impressed with Rudolf. Their personal relationship lasted several years, and their friendship, although at times difficult, lasted for the rest of their lives. They would work together on many occasions, and the technical and artistic influence they had on each other was immensely important for male dancers everywhere. They shared ideas about ways to develop full-length ballets so that the male dancer was placed on an equal footing with the ballerina. Over the years, their individual productions forced audiences to look at male dancers with fresh eyes. Rudolf explained, "I leave everything that is important for ballerinas, but recreate balance by adding solos for men. In this way, I am able to restore rightful role of male dancer in classical ballet."

It was at this same time that Rudolf was introduced to another person who would be an enormous influence in his life — Margot Fonteyn. Vera Volkova had been one of the first instructors of Fonteyn, Britain's reigning ballerina, and the two women had become good friends. One evening, while Rudolf was visiting Volkova's apartment, Fonteyn telephoned from London. Volkova summoned Rudolf to the phone. "It's Margot Fonteyn here," a voice said. "Would you dance in my gala in London? It's to be in October at Drury Lane." He felt honored by the invitation.

Fonteyn arranged for travel documents to help Rudolf enter England, and then invited him to stay with her. Within a few days of their telephone conversation, he flew to London to meet her. The ballerina, who was nineteen years older than Rudolf, was very gracious, and he felt comfortable with her from the beginning. She lived in luxury with her diplomat husband, Roberto "Tito" Arias, the Panamanian ambassador to Great Britain, but despite her stardom and her lofty social position, Rudolf found her to be very "down-to-earth." In his autobiography, he wrote, "From the first moment, I knew I had found a friend."

During Rudolf's first visit, Fonteyn was appearing in *Giselle* at the Covent Garden Opera House, and she made plans for her friends Maude and Nigel Gosling to take him to see the performance. Nigel Gosling was a highly respected art critic, and his beautiful and elegant wife, Maude Lloyd, was a former ballerina. Together, they wrote about dance under the name Alexander Bland. As he had with the Pushkins in Leningrad, Rudolf would "adopt" the Goslings as his "parents in the West." Nigel would also become his intellectual and cultural mentor. And it was with the Goslings (as Alexander Bland) that Rudolf wrote an autobiography the year after he defected.

The Goslings had been in Paris during the Kirov's tour, and had already seen Rudolf dance. When they'd returned to London, they told friends about the young Russian whose dancing had bowled them over. Now, only months later, they were taking Rudolf to see Fonteyn dance. Although the production of *Giselle* was different from the one he'd known in Leningrad, Rudolf took great pleasure in watching Fonteyn's touching performance. He also was impressed by the high standards of

Nigel and Maude Gosling, Rudolf's friends, supporters, and surrogate parents. "Nigel and Maude were like my family, a foundation stone in my life."

the Royal Ballet and thought that it would be an excellent company with which to dance.

Fonteyn introduced him to the founder and director of the Royal Ballet, Ninette de Valois, and to Sir Frederick Ashton, the famous British choreographer. It was agreed that for Rudolf's Drury Lane gala appearance, Ashton would create an original solo dance for him. Rudolf's career in London would be launched by *Poème Tragique,* set to the music of the Russian composer Alexander Scriabin.

Soon after they met, Ashton and Rudolf began rehearsing *Poème Tragique.* Watching Rudolf work filled the other dancers with amazement. They had never seen such energy or effort. Fonteyn stopped in at the first rehearsal, and in her autobiography she described Rudolf as being intensely serious and determined. "From time to time he stopped to take

*Nigel Gosling and Rudolf,
possibly at work on the
manuscript for Rudolf's
autobiography.*

off his leg warmers before a very difficult step; after the exertion he
stopped again, let out a breath rapidly and forcefully with a sound like a
sibilant 'Ho.' On went the woollen tights. After a few more steps he
changed his shoes and put the leg warmers back on top of the woollen
tights. So it went for two hours. He was working like a steam engine."
Ashton also was impressed. "Rudolf," he would later say, "I would give
up everything that I have created just to feel in my body, for five minutes,
what you must feel like in your body every time you dance."

The excitement about this great new dancer set London on fire. His
debut on November 2, 1961, at the Theatre Royal at Drury Lane, electrified the audience. He was cheered for the new solo, and with his partner,
Rosella Hightower, a much-admired American ballerina, he triumphed
in the Black Swan pas de deux. Although his performance was not tech-

nically perfect, his effortless leaps and the passion in his every step whipped the audience into a frenzy. He had conquered Paris. Now London was at his feet.

Watching from the wings, Fonteyn knew that she had to dance with this young man. "I had better get on the bandwagon or else get out," she said to herself. Ninette de Valois came to the same conclusion, and years later would describe the impression he made: "His entry into the West was like a bomb dropped into the ballet world!" Without delay, she invited Rudolf to dance with the Royal Ballet the following February.

Until that arrangement could be finalized, Rudolf decided to join with Bruhn, Hightower, and Sonia Arova, another renowned ballerina, to give a few concerts in France. They danced two performances in Cannes and were to dance another two in Paris. Just before the last performance, however, Bruhn injured his foot. He was able to manage some of the dancing that evening, but not the quick and brilliant footwork demanded by Bournonville's *Flower Festival* pas de deux. Rudolf quickly learned the steps and replaced him, in addition to dancing his own roles. Only days later, Bruhn was scheduled to dance the same pas de deux in New York City with Maria Tallchief. They had been invited to perform on the prestigious television program "The Bell Telephone Hour." Again, Rudolf would fill in.

Although Rudolf had only a few days in New York City, he was determined to make the most of every minute. He was particularly anxious to meet the choreographer and dancer Martha Graham. In London, the Goslings had shown him films of this pioneer of modern dance, and her dancing fascinated him. The worlds of classical ballet and modern dance were far apart in those days, but Rudolf paid no attention to that great divide; he recognized Graham's genius. As soon as he landed in New York, he dashed to the theater in which she was performing.

Rudolf and Bruhn relaxing on the French Riviera, circa 1962.

Unfortunately, however, his trans-Atlantic flight had been especially stormy, and Rudolf was terrified of air travel even at the best of times. Jet-lagged and ill, he was unable to stay until the end of the performance, and he missed meeting her.

He also desperately wanted to meet George Balanchine during that first New York trip. Balanchine had been born in Russia and, like Rudolf, had graduated from the Maryinsky School. Later, he had been a member of the ballet company in Leningrad, as well as of Diaghilev's Ballets Russes. He had also been one of Diaghilev's principal choreographers in the last years of the company, and had created both *Apollo* and *Prodigal Son* for the Ballets Russes. A few years after Diaghilev's death, the writer and art impresario Lincoln Kirstein brought Balanchine to the

United States. He and Kirstein first co-founded the School of American Ballet, and then, in 1948, a company that eventually became known as the New York City Ballet.

Rudolf admired Balanchine and hoped that he might work with him. But the great choreographer did not have the same desire to collaborate with the new star. Balanchine always said, "My company is a company of dancing, not a company of stars." He told Rudolf, "My ballets are too dry for you. Go and dance your princes. When you are tired of them, come back." Rudolf would later joke, "I tried to get those princes out of my system, but they just wouldn't go away!"

Decades later, Rudolf told me that in his mind, Balanchine and Graham were the most important choreographers of the twentieth century. "There have been many great choreographers," he explained. "What makes Balanchine and Graham the greatest . . . is that they changed the direction of both dance and choreography. There have been many others who have created supreme works of dance; however, Balanchine and Graham created revolutions."

Since Rudolf's defection only seven months before, he had enjoyed one success after another. Naturally, he was greatly disappointed that Balanchine was not yet prepared to work with him. But he hoped that the great choreographer would change his mind after seeing him dance. And in the meantime, he had to prepare for his North American debut.

On January 19, 1962, Rudolf's first American performance was broadcast into the living rooms of a vast television audience. That night, he made an unforgettable impression on millions of viewers, including many who had never attended a ballet. Those few thrilling minutes on television sparked a tremendous interest in dance — and created an audience hungry to see more of Nureyev. That enthusiasm for him never diminished in America, and he danced to full theaters there for the rest of his life.

Although Rudolf had fallen in love with New York, he had to return to London to prepare for his first performance with his new partner, Margot Fonteyn. What he didn't yet realize was that with that partnership, a new and important chapter in ballet history was about to be written.

6

RUDIMANIA

When he dances, his offhanded grace burns itself into the memory.
— Clive Barnes

With his move to London, Rudolf was caught up in a whirlwind. His defection had made him an instant celebrity, and he could not go anywhere without being recognized. Hailed as the new Nijinsky, he was stopped on the street for his autograph even by people who had never seen him dance. During this time, he was staying with Fonteyn and Arias in the Panamanian embassy. Although the residence was much grander than the Pushkins' small apartment, the living arrangements were similar and shielded him from the outside world. Once again, the practical details of daily life — namely, cooking, laundry, and shopping — were handled for Rudolf by others. He was free to concentrate on his dancing.

At the center of Rudolf's life were his rehearsals in the Royal Ballet studios. Ninette de Valois, the company's director, had invited him to dance three performances of *Giselle* with Fonteyn. De Valois was a wise woman with tremendous experience, and she had correctly surmised that the sensational young dancer would be good for business. But even she was shocked by the frenzy for tickets, which was so great that all the seats

With Fonteyn in Sir Frederick Ashton's Marguerite and Armand. *The choreographer insisted that this ballet never be performed by anyone else.*

were sold immediately and, according to the Covent Garden box-office staff, another seventy thousand could have been added.

Of course, Londoners were excited not just about seeing Rudolf dance, but about seeing him dance with their beloved Fonteyn. Still, the partnership seemed an unlikely one. It would be hard to imagine two more different people than the ladylike English ballerina and the fiery Tatar. Their backgrounds, personalities, training methods, and styles of dance were completely opposed. Where she was serene, radiant, and experienced, he was passionate, explosive, and instinctive. Where she sparkled, he burned. And to top it all off, he was just twenty-three years old and at the beginning of his career, while Fonteyn was forty-two and nearing retirement. Yet together they shared a rare bond that created magic and perfect harmony.

At first, Fonteyn worried that a partnership with a man as young as Rudolf would look ridiculous. "I was afraid that it would look like mutton dancing with lamb," she told friends half-jokingly. But she was so inspired by his talent that she decided to put her qualms aside. Rudolf had no such reservations about dancing with her. He admired her as a ballerina, and he had already shared a successful partnership in the Soviet Union with Natalia Dudinskaya, who was older than Fonteyn.

Nevertheless, there were some challenges. The two stars were used to dancing very different versions of *Giselle.* As a result, they had to adapt their steps and even their acting to each other. But Rudolf said that the adjustments seemed to come easily. "From the first, I could work with Margot with complete understanding. Though she was a great dancer with enormous experience, she accepted my ideas as though we were on a level playing field."

Those who saw that first performance, whether they watched from the audience or the wings, knew they were witnessing history being made. Excitement swept through the theater like a tidal wave. When the curtain finally fell, the audience went wild. The two dancers received twenty-

From act 2 of Giselle *with the Royal Ballet. Rudolf as Albrecht, Fonteyn (kneeling) as Giselle, and Monica Mason as the Queen of the Wilis. One of the greatest partnerships in ballet history was formed on February 21, 1962, when Rudolf and Fonteyn performed their first* Giselle.

three curtain calls. In an unplanned moment during one, Fonteyn lovingly gave Rudolf a rose from her bouquet. Rudolf fell to one knee, bowed his head, and tenderly kissed her hand. His emotional gesture propelled the audience to a fever pitch. Although others would later copy the famous bow, Fonteyn thought it emphasized the age difference between the two of them. After that performance, she insisted on curtsying to Rudolf instead.

On that night, February 21, 1962, one of the greatest partnerships in ballet was created. The reviews were filled with rapturous praise. Mary Clarke wrote in the *Sunday Times,* "We have come to think of ballet partnerships as being made in the classroom and over years on the stage of patiently working together, but on Wednesday we learned that they are

Rudolf once said, "In Eugene Onegin, *the Russian poet Aleksandr Pushkin wrote, 'From the overflow of soul, a dancer flies.' I believe he was saying that dance has a meaning equal to poetry when it is spiritually inspired. It is not just your technical ability to do steps, you must find meaning in every movement you do."*

made in heaven." The esteemed critic Clive Barnes wrote, referring to Rudolf, "His genius outstrips his talent; when he dances, his offhanded grace burns itself into the memory."

Ninette de Valois saw that Fonteyn and Rudolf were meant to dance together. And she also realized that Rudolf, with his Kirov training, had much to teach her dancers. She desperately wanted him to join the Royal Ballet, but in those days only citizens of the British Commonwealth could be members. The resourceful de Valois found a solution. Despite some criticism, she invited Rudolf to join the company as a permanent guest artist.

Rudolf was profoundly influenced by the Royal Ballet during his years there. He not only was given a home base, which is so important for a young dancer who is still developing, but was also able to refine his technique, especially his footwork. De Valois even gave him the chance to stage his own productions, beginning with *La Bayadère* in 1963, and followed by *Raymonda* in 1964 and *The Nutcracker* in 1968. Most meaningful for Rudolf, however, were the many ballets choreographed specially for him. These included *Ropes of Time* by Rudi van Dantzig, *Paradise Lost* by Roland Petit, *Laborintus* by Glen Tetley, and several ballets by Sir Kenneth MacMillan.

The most famous of the ballets choreographed for Rudolf and Margot Fonteyn was *Marguerite and Armand.* Sir Frederick Ashton based the ballet on the Alexandre Dumas novel *Lady of the Camelias,* which tells the story of two star-crossed lovers. (The book was also the basis for Verdi's opera *La Traviata.*) Ashton created this passionate work as a tribute to their extraordinary partnership, and he insisted that it never be performed by any other dancers. In her autobiography, Fonteyn wrote that preceding the opening night, the press implied that there might be a powerful true-life love story between the two lead dancers. She insisted the rumors were false, but it all added to the excitement. *Marguerite and Armand* would become their "signature piece."

For his part, Rudolf also made several important contributions to the Royal Ballet. He served as a model to a generation of very talented young male dancers. For men such as Anthony Dowell, David Wall, and Wayne Sleep — as well as others who followed later, such as Wayne Eagling and Stephen Jeffries — he was a shining example. Always generous with his knowledge, he introduced technical fireworks into their vocabulary of steps. He challenged them to be less restrained in their approach, always pushing them to be more physical and sensual. Whenever he could, he would offer encouragement, often helping others in class and in rehearsals. This encouragement also extended to many of the younger ballerinas he partnered, including Lynn Seymour, Antoinette Sibley, Merle Park, and Monica Mason.

He also made a contribution through the many productions he staged for the Royal Ballet. The productions themselves were generally successful both financially and artistically, enriching the already extensive repertoire of the company, and they gave the Russian-trained dancer the opportunity to coach his colleagues in what was a new style for them.

And, of course, the company benefited from the fanfare surrounding the partnership of Fonteyn and Nureyev. By pushing each other to new personal heights, the two dancers set the standard by which all subsequent partnerships would be judged. Alexander Bland wrote, "Their partnership produced performances that have changed the course of ballet history."

The public's excitement over their appearances brought greater attention to ballet all around the world. In fact, this was the beginning of the so-called ballet boom. Everywhere Rudolf and Fonteyn danced, fans lined up for days to buy tickets, often camping out in sleeping bags and tents in all kinds of weather to ensure that they got their seats.

One of their fans, Sandy Perry, remembers lining up in the rain outside the Covent Garden box office. Inside the theater, Fonteyn and Rudolf were rehearsing *Romeo and Juliet*. The ballerina said, "Rudolf, it's dreadful outside. I'm going to go to the canteen and bring those poor fans some coffee and doughnuts. They must be soaked to the skin!" Rudolf replied, "Margot, fans be happier with you if you stay here and rehearse and make perfect performance." She stayed to finish the rehearsal, but afterwards took hot drinks to the grateful fans and, with her characteristic good humor, told them what had been discussed inside.

Fonteyn had already been a major star when Rudolf was just a boy. In fact, she had danced her first *Swan Lake* a few months before Rudolf was born. But it was their partnership that catapulted them both to super-stardom. Invitations to dance poured in from around the world. They were asked to perform at special galas before royalty and world leaders, and at the White House for the inauguration of President Lyndon Johnson in 1965.

Photos began appearing of the two dining in restaurants or dancing in discotheques with celebrities. In 1964, when they performed the premiere of Rudolf's production of *Swan Lake* for the Vienna State Opera Ballet, they received eighty-nine curtain calls, an accomplishment that earned them a place in the *Guinness Book of World Records* and has never been surpassed.

With all that attention, some bad publicity was sure to appear. One of the most sensational stories came out of San Francisco in 1967, when both dancers had been invited to a party by some fans. Soon after the stars arrived, the house was raided by the police, who were searching for marijuana. Rudolf and Fonteyn never smoked cigarettes, much less took drugs, but they were caught trying to flee and were arrested. Even though all the charges were dropped immediately, the story made headline news around the world.

Rudolf had been arrested once before, when he took a late-night walk in Toronto after a performance in 1963. It was three in the morning, and his walk included a bit of dancing up the center line of the city's famous Yonge Street. When a policeman ordered him home, Rudolf ignored him and continued dancing. The officer told him he was under arrest. But Rudolf said, "You cannot arrest me. I'm Rudolf Nureyev." The policemen responded, "Yeah, and I'm Fred Astaire — but *you* are under arrest!" Rudolf was handcuffed and taken to the police station. The next morning, the charges were dismissed, but the gossip-seeking media still made a sensation of it. One report even claimed that he had been "arrested in the middle of the night for leaping over cars."

Rudolf and Fonteyn during a curtain call for Swan Lake. *Alexander Bland wrote, "Their partnership produced performances that changed the course of ballet history."*

Every move Rudolf made both onstage and off earned him space in magazines and newspapers. The media especially reveled in stories about his famously explosive temper. It was well known that he could be charming one minute and rude the next, and more than one writer referred to him as the "Tatar Tiger" because of both his fiery temperament and the catlike quality of his dancing. He was mentioned in the fashion sections because of his flamboyant clothes, and his long locks attracted attention even before the Beatles made hair a topic of controversy. Rudolf had become the center of the whirlwind that was London in the 1960s. It was the time of the "youthquake," when restless young Londoners were challenging many of society's conventions and traditions. The pendulum had been set in motion by the Beatles, with their smart-aleck attitudes and their fresh music. Thanks to them, everything English was cool. Carnaby Street colors, Twiggy's impossibly thin frame, and Mary Quant's miniskirts set the style for "with it" people everywhere from Hong Kong to Milwaukee.

Rudolf was not only part of the scene — he defined it. He was talented, he was young, he was exotically attractive, and he was rebellious. Everywhere he turned, ballet's superstar was dogged by the media — so much so that the press dubbed the frenzy "Rudimania." In the single week of April 16, 1965, Rudolf appeared on the covers of both *Newsweek* and *Time.*

Rudolf had a shrewd understanding of his media value, and although the publicity often annoyed him, he realized that it was his best protection against the KGB. He knew he was in real danger of being whisked off the street by the secret police, drugged, and taken back to the Soviet Union, especially in the first few years after his defection. It had happened to other former citizens, and he knew it could happen to him, too. Sometimes, while walking down the street, he'd feel like he was being followed and would hail the first available taxi to help him escape. On several occasions, I heard him tell people that he remained constantly in the headlines so that his disappearance, if it happened, would become an international incident. "So," he would scoff, "I let press use me, and cleverly, I use press!"

Rudolf's lifelong drive to control his own circumstances extended to the way he used the media and even, to a lesser degree, to Rudimania. Of course, the Rudimania frenzy created more opportunities for him than he could use. But he crammed every possible performance, every possible chance to choreograph, and every possible occasion to travel into every single day. "Seize life by the throat," he advised his colleagues. "You must grab every opportunity and then make it count."

7

A PERFORMANCE DAY

Audiences come to theater to see people obsessed by what they do!
— Rudolf Nureyev

Even at the height of Rudimania, the man at the center of it all never seemed to lose his footing or his sense of perspective. He saw himself, first and always, as a working dancer. And he never became dependent on the press or his fans to help him judge how well he had danced — he was his own toughest critic.

Wherever he was appearing throughout the long years of his career, Rudolf followed a similar pattern on his performance days. The day started with class, even if he was tired, injured, or ill. Though he was a professional dancer for many years, and had over those years taken thousands of classes, he never treated his exercises in a matter-of-fact manner. Sergiu Stefanschi, who was reunited with Rudolf in the National Ballet of Canada, observed, "He never stopped examining his technique, studying, and improving. He was always a student."

When Rudolf joined the National Ballet of Canada, we learned quickly that he had very definite ideas about how a class should be constructed. He asked our teachers to give very slow barre work, for example. He used these early exercises almost as massage for his tired muscles —

Rehearsing the daisy scene in Giselle *with Canada's Karen Kain. Ballerinas Veronica Tennant and Vanessa Harwood are practicing in the background.*

Rudolf in class with Georgina Parkinson and members of the Royal Ballet.

extending and pliéing with great care and concentration. All the while, he worked on creating a more elegant line. He also asked that certain exercises be repeated or made longer, both at the barre and in the center work. For instance, Rudolf spent much time on the slow adagio work. When he taught class himself, his adagio exercises could be agonizingly long. He believed that long adagio exercises gave us the strength to stand securely on one leg, the control required to land from a jump holding a clean position, and the power to end the most energetic solos with frozen stillness.

Of all the steps in ballet, pirouettes, those fast-spinning turns on one leg, were the most troublesome for Rudolf. Those who saw him dance, or who have seen films of his performances, would be surprised to know how much difficulty he had, because he turns well and finishes cleanly. But his mastery of pirouettes was a matter of old-fashioned hard work.

He also made continual, concentrated efforts to polish his footwork. Over the years, he incorporated into his technique the neat leg and footwork training of both the English and the Danish schools. As a result, his batterie (leg beats) and footwork were spectacular. Mikhail Baryshnikov, who (with Nureyev, Erik Bruhn, and Vaslav Nijinsky) is considered one of the greatest male dancers of the twentieth century, has said that Rudolf had a way of drawing the audience's attention to the precision of his legs and feet — so much so that Baryshnikov called them Rudolf's talking legs.

Rehearsals followed class, and he continued to push his body, which he sometimes called his battleground. Rudolf possessed a wonderful and impish sense of humor. During rehearsals, he often poked fun at himself with rude jokes about his own technical and physical shortcomings. Those moments of clowning around lightened what was usually an atmosphere of intense concentration.

Rudolf was also an exceptional and generous teacher. He watched the struggles of other dancers and coached us by example or by conjuring up images for us. Sometimes a single word from him captured the essence of a problem and showed us how to correct it. It was not enough for him that you could execute a step; you had to do it with full commitment. "Try to find impulse of movement," he directed. "It is that impulse that gives attack and interest. Find impulse, then force into shape and into rhythm. There *must* be a reason behind *every movement* you do."

One of my favorite directions was when he commanded, "Dance boldly and full out. Hold back nothing! Timid is not interesting! If you are timid, you will be eaten up by costumes and stage scenery. Take the stage and command it! You have talent, now let it possess you! Audiences come to theater to see people obsessed by what they do!"

This warm, generous man was not the Rudolf we had expected when he first joined our company. We all had heard for years about his towering rages and his legendary Tatar temper. I suppose we were lucky — by the time he danced with us, he had mellowed somewhat. But that is not to say that we did not sometimes feel his anger simmering just below the surface. He displayed his fury on occasion, but it was usually short lived. With us, Rudolf routinely showed a quiet patience while looking for ways to help us refine our dancing.

"He was always pushing us to dig deeper for ways to improve ourselves," remembered Mikko Nissinen, a Finnish dancer whom Rudolf admired for both his skill and his intellectual curiosity. In fact, Rudolf often did the digging, not just for himself but also for others. The National Ballet's Veronica Tennant recalled that Rudolf had not known exactly how to help her in her struggle with the famous — and treacherous — attitude balances in the Rose Adagio of *Sleeping Beauty.* But one morning he rushed excitedly up to her and said, "I called Margot last night for advice for you, and she suggested you try strength of balance in shoulders rather than thinking of balances from toes." Tennant gratefully observed, "This proved to be the key, and before every performance I blessed both Margot and Rudolf for it!"

With Luigi Pignotti. Rudolf became so reliant on Pignotti, his masseur and close friend, that he eventually asked him to produce and manage some of his later tours.

After rehearsals and lunch, Rudolf spent his afternoons browsing in stores for antiques, rare maps, and books, or visiting museums or art galleries. On occasion, he had his chauffeur take him for a long drive. He was always on the lookout for new sights, sounds, and ideas to weave into his work. When he returned to his hotel, he attended to his schedule of engagements or to his business affairs. Although he had an excellent agent in Sandor Gorlinsky, he often made his own bookings, especially if there was a performance he desperately wanted to do. Then came his nap, a light meal, and a pre-performance massage by his masseur, Luigi Pignotti. With such a grueling schedule, his daily massages were a necessity. Beginning in the early 1970s, Pignotti acted not only as Rudolf's masseur, but also as manager of his everyday needs. He came to know Rudolf as well as anyone, understanding his fears, superstitions, and eccentricities, as well as his likes and dislikes. Over time, he became one of Rudolf's most trusted friends.

On arriving at the theater before a performance, Rudolf would go straight to his dressing room to apply his makeup. When he was dancing with Fonteyn, she would sometimes bring her makeup into his dressing room so that they could talk and laugh together while they got ready. He often used this time to speak with friends, fellow dancers, and even reporters.

Unlike many dancers, Rudolf did not seem to have too many dressing-room superstitions. People who work on the stage often have unusual habits or strange beliefs that come out of theatrical tradition. For instance, no one would think of whistling in a theater. In less technological times, the rigging of curtains and backdrops was based on the rigging of ships. Stagehands used whistles as cues, in much the same way as sailors used whistles as signals to change the sails. An absentminded performer's whistle, therefore, could cause havoc for those onstage.

Rudolf's strongest theatrical superstition had to do with his ballet shoes. He never gave his slippers away — not to friends, not to colleagues, not to charities to raise funds. It was if he felt that giving away his shoes would be like giving away a piece of his soul. On tour, he carried with him a suitcase full of shoes, some brand new and others repeatedly patched and nearly worn out. I seem to remember Rudolf always wearing the ones that were the most worn.

Rudolf had other superstitions. His most well-known ones involved the numbers thirteen and seventeen. In his mind, seventeen signified good fortune and thirteen bad fortune. If by chance thirteen people ended up seated at a dinner table, Rudolf would insist that we either add

Rudolf applying makeup in his dressing room with just a few of the many ballet slippers he always carried with him. Although Rudolf had only a handful of superstitions, he rarely threw his slippers away, even when they became worn and tattered.

someone to the gathering or ask someone to leave. By contrast, the number seventeen figured in several happy events in his life: he was born on the seventeenth of March; he was seventeen when the Leningrad Ballet School accepted him; and, he claimed, it was the seventeenth of August when he traveled to his audition for the school.

Unfortunately for those who worked with him, Rudolf's superstitions did not extend to getting ready well in advance of a performance. On the contrary, he seemed to make himself late on purpose in order to get his adrenaline flowing. In the process, he created a small tempest around himself. Some people took offense to his outbursts, but most of us knew just to stay clear and let Rudolf get ready in his own way.

After applying his makeup, he would proceed to the side of the stage to warm up. If he was not to appear until later in the performance, he would set his ballet barre close to the wings so that he could watch the other dancers onstage while he did his exercises. Whether he was warming up or in the middle of his own performance, he always kept an eye on his fellow dancers. As we came off the stage, he sometimes beckoned us over to give us a correction or make a suggestion, an infinitely generous act from a dancer who was also concentrating on his own work.

While we performed, it was exhilarating to glimpse Rudolf standing in the wings and encouraging us to push ourselves beyond our own limitations. Occasionally, he would bark some correction at us while we were in mid-act. Those corrections were almost always accompanied by a swear word or two in any one of the several languages he spoke. Nevertheless, most dancers were pleased by his attention and considered his comments to be gifts; we all understood how much he wanted us to succeed.

Once in a while, a performance was delayed because Rudolf was injured and needed extra time to prepare. One night in Chicago, he was having difficulty warming up a torn calf muscle. The theater manager paced back and forth, while on the other side of the curtain the clapping of the impatient audience grew louder and louder. Infuriated, Rudolf stormed to the edge of the stage, parted the front curtain, and yelled, "Everyone shut up!" Like naughty children who had just been told to hush and behave, the audience obeyed. Minutes later, the overture began and the crowd was treated to a glorious performance. During the intermission, a patron remarked to her friends that she did not know which was more memorable – seeing Nureyev dance or witnessing one of his famous tantrums.

Rudolf and Lucette Aldous flying in grand jetés in Rudolf's production of Don Quixote *with the Australian Ballet.*

Every performance has its risks, and occasionally a night can go terribly wrong. Most theater people live by the creed that no matter what, the show must go on. Rudolf believed this, but he also thought that an audience was entitled to see a great performance. If there was a disaster that could not be covered up or that would ruin a production, he felt it was wrong to pretend that nothing had happened. To ignore it was to cheat the audience.

One such calamity occurred when he was touring with the Australian Ballet. One evening, during his own production of *Don Quixote,* Rudolf slipped in the middle of a variation and ended up flat on his back like a turtle. Accidents can happen to any dancer, but in this case Rudolf was partly to blame. Like Pavlova before him, he hated dancing on floors that were covered by linoleum. Whenever possible, he preferred to dance on a wooden stage. In that particular theater, the stage was very slippery, but Rudolf had refused to let the ballet company put down its linoleum flooring. This was what had caused him to fall.

Pulling himself up from the floor, he signaled to the conductor to stop the orchestra. In silence, he strutted off the stage and into the wings to rub resin on his shoes. The audience sat stock-still, and the dancers onstage remained frozen in their positions. The only sounds to be heard in the theater were Rudolf's shoes shuffling in the resin box and a tirade of swear words. Everyone nervously waited to see what the temperamental dancer would do next.

Then, as if nothing had happened, Rudolf grandly re-entered from the wings. With wide, self-assured strides and a defiant expression on his face, he started his solo from the beginning. This time, everything went perfectly, and at the end of the solo the audience cheered with excitement.

Whether Rudolf entered at the start or in the middle of a ballet, his first appearance raised the level of excitement on both sides of the footlights. As soon as he emerged, people unconsciously leaned toward him, as if pulled by a magnet. But beforehand, Rudolf, like all performers, could be nervous. Although he never revealed his stage fright to the audience, there were a few clues in the darkened backstage wings. I could tell when he was particularly nervous, because when he took my hand to lead me onstage, his would be as cold as ice. At other times, he'd push past us with a cavalier "Well, off to slaughter!" To counter our own nervousness, he'd say, "We dancers are paid to control our nerves," or, quoting Mark Twain, "Courage is not the lack of fear — it is having fear and then conquering it!"

Despite these occasional bouts of stage fright, Rudolf was happiest when he was onstage. He took pleasure in feeling the warm glow of the spotlight on his face. He loved the exchange of energy with the audience and the camaraderie of working with other dancers. Most of all, he loved the pure physical joy of dancing.

His dancing was truly the essence of Rudolf the person — powerful yet vulnerable, fiery yet romantic, and always analytically intelligent. He had tremendous technical prowess, of course, but his movements also had an unusually graceful, soft quality. He was not feminine, he was fluid. His arm and hand movements were especially beautiful. The distinguished dance writer Doris Hering noted, "He can do a simple port de bras [movement of the arms], and by its breadth and timing make it the most important gesture ever to illuminate the stage."

He was a true classical prince. But unlike other great princes, such as Erik Bruhn, Anthony Dowell, and Laurent Hilaire, Rudolf did not have an effortless look to his dancing. When he ran, for instance, he seemed to tear up the floor under his feet. We would stand in the wings, shake our heads in amazement, and joke, "There goes tiger paws." And he leaped with the fierceness of a jungle cat. He was like a tightly coiled spring that, when released, flies unimpeded through the air.

As Rudolf always pointed out to us, however, "It is not how *high* you jump in air. It is *how* you present it." In his case, not only did his leaps soar, but, as Margot Fonteyn said, "He seemed to defy gravity by hovering for a moment in the air." She thought that his corkscrew jumps in the solo from *Le Corsaire* "looked exactly as though he was flying on an invisible magic carpet."

Almost as remarkable as Rudolf's legendary leaps was his ability to land from a jump and not move a muscle. To hurtle through space and then stop suddenly and hold the pose, elegantly and in frozen stillness, takes immense control. The effect was thrilling. When he coached us,

Rudolf insisted that we sustain our landings with the same stillness and with our heels firmly down. "Use floor when jumping. Lift up from it. And when you land, let it hold you."

He was a master of stagecraft and stillness. Even when he was utterly motionless, with his back turned to the audience, he had the magnetism of a wild animal. No one could stand onstage and command attention the way he could. One reviewer said it perfectly — "His power was absolute."

He was also intensely musical, although reviewers sometimes criticized him as both a dancer and a choreographer for toying with established interpretations and musical phrasings. He admitted that one of his great musical influences was the popular entertainer Fred Astaire. "His important discovery, I think, is that dancer doesn't have to be slave to music," Rudolf observed. "He imposed his own rhythms, his own phrasing on the music, like another instrument in the orchestration."

Although we received wonderful instruction from Rudolf in class and rehearsals, it was by performing with him that we learned the most. He never cheated by making steps easier for himself. Instead, he constantly challenged himself by making his solos more and more difficult.

Dancing with him was thrilling. As a partner, he was generous and instinctive, and although he was only 5 foot 8, he was powerfully secure. When Rudolf extended his hand in an invitation to dance with him, he looked you straight in the eye with an expression of daring. You could feel him commanding you to dance your best. You knew that he would be there for you, especially in your most dangerous moments, because he gave his partner the same focused attention he gave his own solos. There was a romantic passion about him, and a sensuality that moved his audiences and his partners alike.

Among the many lessons he taught his younger and less experienced partners was how to believe in themselves. In her autobiography, Karen

Rudolf's curtain calls were as legendary as his dancing.

Kain wrote, "People used to say Rudolf discovered me — the truth is that he helped me discover myself. His demand that I meet and exceed his expectations, coupled with his certainty that I could do so, enabled me to dance far better than I imagined possible."

Rudolf shared an extraordinary rapport not only with his partners, but also with his audiences. His legendary curtain calls were like an additional last act of the ballet — sometimes a very long last act. He would lead his ballerina in front of the curtain, where they were greeted with booming applause and a shower of bouquets. Occasionally, a bouquet would come hurling toward his face like a missile. Seeing it out of the corner of his eye, he would extend one arm like a baseball player and snatch it out of midair without bothering to turn his head. Delighted, the crowd would laugh and hoot with approval.

For his solo bow, he would walk slowly in front of the curtain and stand perfectly still in the spotlight. Eventually, he would acknowledge the wild cheering with a courtly bow from the waist. As the applause and bravos continued, he would extend his right arm to the right-hand side of the auditorium. There, the audience members would shout and applaud even louder. He would repeat the same gesture to the left, with the same effect. Finally, he would lift both arms toward the balconies and the whole theater would explode in a deafening chorus of bravos, as if it was the audience's turn to play a role in the events of the evening. Rudolf loved the ritual and so did they.

At the end of a performance, Rudolf would change into his street clothes and emerge to meet friends and well-wishers. He was especially kind to the relatives of fellow dancers whenever they were introduced. He understood the sacrifices a family had to make to help a dancer become a professional, and he admired the support parents gave to their children. He often wished his own parents had given him such encouragement.

Leaving the stage door at the Metropolitan Opera House surrounded by fans. At times, Rudolf worried that members of the KGB had infiltrated the crowd.

As he left the theater, Rudolf was usually blockaded by a sea of fans. One of his great admirers, Lynn Perry, remembers, "He was the most generous of performers with his fans. Night after night, year after year, country after country, injured or tired, he would make time for those who supported him. Rudolf would plow into his crowd of well-wishers, thanking us for our praise, joking, signing autographs, or speaking a few words to a nervous and hopeful child. It was a nightly ritual that sometimes lasted for half an hour." Rudolf was well aware of the risks of making himself so available to his fans. On occasion, he worried that the KGB might infiltrate the crowds around him. And the worry that one of his fans might be a real fanatic was brought home when John Lennon was killed by a fan outside the Dakota building in New York City. That was the same apartment building where Rudolf lived.

Over the years, however, Rudolf came to know many of his fans, and a handful even worked for him. At first, he had found it difficult to understand their intense devotion. He wondered how they could afford so many tickets and how they managed to travel to so many different cities to see his performances. Eventually, though, he came to deeply appreciate their devotion and even looked for familiar faces in the front rows. At the end of his career, when he no longer danced as well and the critics savaged his performances, he saw many of his longtime fans in the theater and observed, "They have always stood by me."

Onstage, Rudolf gave so much of himself that he used the hours afterward to unwind. "Performances are like celebration — with dinner, we continue celebration!" he would declare, sweeping us into his limousine. For dinner, he would usually begin with soup, then follow that with a very rare steak, salad, and potatoes. His steak order was specific. "Bring it blue," he directed, "but inside must be warm to touch of tongue." When the order was not prepared to his liking, the exacting Rudolf would send it back to the kitchen, sometimes more than once.

Every meal for Rudolf ended with tea. He drank tea with lemon and a lot of sugar all day long. Fresh pots were kept in his dressing room and in the backstage wings for him during performances. He liked to joke, "I have tea to wake me up. I have tea to go to sleep. I have tea to get me excited and to calm me down. Sometimes I even drink tea when I am thirsty."

When Rudolf performed in the major cities of the world, his dinner companions often included other stars and celebrities. He usually invited fellow dancers to join him, because he felt it was important for us to meet accomplished people from outside our narrow world of dance. But he had high expectations for those he took under his wing. We were expected to hold our own in conversation and to make the most of the opportunity. Those who did not, and had to be baby-sat, were unlikely to be included again.

Rudolf was generous with his knowledge, his time, and even his money when it came to helping a young dancer further his or her education. He always encouraged us to listen, watch, learn, and read. He possessed a limitless curiosity, and he knew from his own experience that a person could educate himself. He insisted that talent alone was not enough to make an artist — a true creator needed a questioning mind and the determination to broaden his knowledge. He told us, "You can have many things taken away from you — your money, your friends, your country, even your health — but never your knowledge. It travels with you everywhere."

After dinner, Rudolf's long day was nearly over. He would return home for a steaming bath and a final massage. Too keyed up to sleep, he would then watch old movies or telephone friends around the world. In the wee hours of the morning, Rudolf would read a book until he dropped off to sleep. His favorite authors included Lord Byron in English, Gustave Flaubert in French, and Aleksandr Pushkin (no relation to his former teacher) in Russian. Then, renewed after only four or five hours of sleep, he would get up the next morning and begin his schedule all over again.

8

THE TATAR NOMAD

I put down roots on the stages of world. My roots are my work.
The stage is my home.
— Rudolf Nureyev

Rudolf believed that his birth aboard a moving train was an omen of the course his life would take. Many times he told journalists, "I am Tatar, not Russian. Traveling is in my blood." The Tatars were feared thirteenth-century nomads who rode on horseback across Asia and Eastern Europe, camped in tents, and conquered people wherever they roamed. In Rudolf's case, he flew around the world, camped out in luxurious accommodations, and conquered people wherever he performed.

In the late 1960s and early 1970s, as Fonteyn danced less and less, Rudolf was offered fewer performances by the Royal Ballet. Eventually, he felt cast aside and was deeply hurt. Even though his popularity had also turned the spotlight on the company's other dancers, many felt overshadowed. And as had been the case when he danced with the Kirov, there were those who resented the special treatment the temperamental dancer received. Rudolf no longer felt welcome.

To satisfy his ravenous hunger to dance, Rudolf — along with Sandor Gorlinsky, his agent, the legendary Sol Hurok, and several other impresarios — filled his calendar with performance engagements and international

The Tatar Nomad.

tours. By some counts, he danced with more than forty different companies. Some writers were critical of those alliances, claiming that the companies were being used as backdrops for Rudolf's gluttonous need to be onstage. The truth is that everyone profited. Many of those companies received invitations to perform in cities and theaters that would not have considered booking them without a superstar like Rudolf on the bill. In addition, his association with those companies gave countless ballerinas and soloists the opportunity to appear with the most famous male dancer of their generation. Many of them received international attention for the first time. For Rudolf, these arrangements allowed him to keep dancing. He would cross the globe again and again, appearing whenever and wherever he could.

During these years, Rudolf was at his physical peak. Night after night, week after week, he performed. He maintained a grueling schedule and appeared on every continent except Antarctica, dancing as many as three hundred performances a year, seven or eight a week. Those of us who worked with him were awed by the demands he made of himself. He performed while ill with high fevers, and even with serious and painful injuries. At times, he danced with not one but both legs bandaged to his knees. He almost never canceled a performance, and he never gave in to fatigue. We called him "Rudolf Never-off." He seemed to be superhuman.

Our company was one of those that danced with Rudolf for three or four months on each tour. One night during a curtain call, after the eighth show of that week, he turned to me and asked if I was tired. Not wanting to admit to exhaustion, I threw the question back to him and asked where he found his enormous strength. Rudolf replied, "Ah! It is basic law of physics! Energy creates energy! The harder I work, the stronger I become, the better I dance." He was right — rather than thinking about how hard work wears you down, why not focus on how it builds you up?

He also believed that his heavy schedule helped him counteract his stage fright. "When I dance only one or two performances a week, I get very nervous," he explained. "On day of show, I die a little bit all day until performance. Nerves drain energy. When I dance eight perform-ances a week, I am best on last performance, because my body knows what it is doing and I am not so nervous." Finally, he advised, "No matter what, push on and learn in process of doing it." Although he often encouraged us with advice like this, it was his own example that truly helped us survive those long and exhausting weeks and months.

Touring with Rudolf was an endurance test. His demand for 100 percent from all concerned — dancers, conductors, wardrobe personnel, and stage crews — was well known in the dance world. Everything about a performance mattered to him, and his attention to detail was amazing. Nothing got past his eagle eyes.

It was equally well known that a company was often at its best when-ever Rudolf appeared on the bill. I believe that those performances were enhanced not just because he inspired his fellow dancers, but also because he improved the physical conditions surrounding them. For instance, he would insist that the stage be washed before every performance and the lights adjusted out of the dancers' eyes. If he was displeased with the positioning of the stage lights, he would push past the stagehands and refocus them himself — sometimes in the middle of a performance.

So that the dancers would have more room, he fought for the sets to be moved as far off the stage as was physically and artistically possible. This was yet another reason why the presence of Rudolf, who as a super-star exerted absolute control, was a blessing for us. We were often ignored when making those same reasonable requests, but it was impos-sible to ignore Rudolf. Nothing ignited his lightening-quick temper faster than the four words "It can't be done." Stage crews quickly learned to honor his requests or face his well-known Tatar temper.

Rudolf, director of the Paris Opéra Ballet, rehearses his dancers with ballet mistress Patricia Ruanne (a former ballerina with the London Festival Ballet) and ballet master Patrice Bart.

When it came to what was best for his art, Rudolf would say, "I make no compromises with myself or with anyone else." He expected everyone around him to live up to their potential, and he was always available with help and encouragement for those who tried. Over and over, he drove us to new heights by commanding, "Nothing happens unless you make it happen — even if you have awesome talent! You must be uncompromising with your talent."

He had no patience for those who were lazy or not serious about their work. With them, he could be brutal and cutting. But for those who strove to do their best, he was a shining example of what could be achieved. The brilliant American star Fernando Bujones remembers, "When I saw Rudi and Margot at the Royal Ballet, I began to have a vision in front of me. I said to myself, 'You know, if Rudi's done it, I can do it.' That was my vision ... Rudi in front of me." For dancers and companies alike, standards rose wherever he appeared. When he was asked why he thought that was, he replied, "I don't know. Maybe I make pot boil at higher temperature."

If ballet's first golden age in the twentieth century was ushered in by Diaghilev's Ballets Russes, Rudolf's flight to the West marked the beginning of a second golden age. But one person cannot be given all the credit for a resurgence of popular interest in an art form. Many new ballet and modern-dance companies and choreographers had emerged since the Second World War. And even before Rudolf's defection, Jacques D'Amboise and Edward Villella, both stars with the New York City Ballet, had captured the public's imagination with their masculine, powerful styles.

All this robust international activity created a new excitement for dance — some called it a dance boom — and Rudolf was in demand all over the world. Not only did he travel to join several ballet companies, some companies even traveled to join him. Once, at the Metropolitan Opera House in New York, he finished a season with the National Ballet of Canada and two days later started his next season with the Royal Ballet. He didn't even have to change his dressing room — when one company moved out of the Met, the other moved in.

Although he appeared extensively in the United States, Rudolf did not have any long-term relationships with the major American ballet companies. He more often performed with foreign ballet companies and American modern-dance companies. To his deep regret, he appeared only once with the New York City Ballet, and that was after George Balanchine died. With American Ballet Theatre, he set the full-length ballet *Raymonda,* but he did not have a close tie with the company (although he did admire ABT's many great dancers — Fernando Bujones, Cynthia Gregory, and Gelsey Kirkland among them).

Rudolf, with Denise Jackson and Christian Holder, in the Joffrey Ballet production of Petrouchka. *"Since the magical appearance of Nijinsky, before the First World War,"* wrote the critic Fernau Hall, *"no male dancer has captured the imagination of millions as Rudolf Nureyev has done."*

Perhaps his most interesting collaboration with an American ballet company was that with the Joffrey Ballet. Together, they mounted an evening to mark the fiftieth anniversary of the death of Serge Diaghilev. It was a difficult undertaking which involved painstakingly reconstructing the choreography of some of Diaghilev's nearly forgotten ballets. The program included Michel Fokine's *Petrouchka* and *Spectre de la Rose*, Vaslav Nijinksy's *Afternoon of a Faun*, and Leonide Massine's *Parade*. In the first three ballets, Rudolf danced the roles Nijinsky had created.

At the Moscow Circus with the author, her husband, and their two sons. Rudolf joked that it was no great coincidence that he was attacked by a tiger at a Russian circus.

With so much time spent traveling and on the stages of the world, Rudolf was bound to suffer the occasional mishap or near catastrophe. In Milwaukee, Wisconsin, a streaker ran across the stage, naked as the day he was born — except for his shoes. In London, Rudolf was struck by a motorcycle. And in Toronto, the Tatar tiger had an encounter with a real Siberian tiger.

It was 1989 and the Moscow Circus was in town. They invited Rudolf to come to their show, and then to go backstage to meet the performers and see the animals. While he was there, Rudolf was asked by the local promoter to pose for a publicity photo holding a tiger on a leash. Just as the picture was snapped, however, a little girl strayed too close and the tiger lunged. Rudolf mustered all his strength to rein in the furious animal, who in response wrapped his sharp claws around Rudolf's calf. Fortunately, the tiger's trainer rushed to help, and together they finally restrained the powerful cat.

As we were riding back to the hotel in his limousine, Rudolf admitted that he had had a real, gut-wrenching fright. And he was furious that a mother would let her child wander so close to the animal. But he recovered from his anger quickly. Later that night, he was able to joke about the incident. "I do not need calves torn from outside, too," he said, referring to the internal tears to his calf muscles that had plagued him for years. Then he noted that he'd been attacked at a *Russian* circus. "I think the KGB is still trying to get me!" he quipped.

Mishaps, calamities, near catastrophes never seemed to phase Rudolf all that much, but there was one fear he never really conquered. As much as he loved exploring new places and dancing with companies all over the world, he was terrified of flying. In typical fashion, however, he did not allow this, his worst fear, to interfere with a single engagement. There were even times when he flew over the ocean for a performance on one continent and flew back the very next day to dance that evening on another.

On airplanes, he often curled up on the seat in fright. He tried to ease his dread by waiting until the last possible moment to decide which plane to take. "I debate endlessly . . . which plane is less likely to kill me." When he had a choice, he would travel through the night in his limousine, sleeping in the backseat while the rest of us flew to the next performance.

Rudolf was also afraid of catching cold. In summer or winter, inside or out, he would bundle himself in scarves, hats, and sweaters. He sweated through class and rehearsals wearing several pairs of leg warmers, one on top of the other. He protected himself from drafts, real and imagined, and air conditioning, which he constantly demanded be turned off. His extreme fear of catching cold seemed eccentric to some, but behind it lay a very real concern about lung ailments, to which he was prone. In 1979, he was hospitalized with pneumonia and missed several performances with American Ballet Theatre. For Rudolf "Never-off," missing even one performance was pure torture.

Rudolf was a man of great contrasts. He enjoyed buying and wearing beautiful and expensive clothes, for example, but when he was on tour he carried only a few changes of clothing — even when those tours kept him on the road for months at a time. Instead of clothes, he filled his suitcases with dozens of pairs of ballet slippers, costumes, books, video- and audiotapes, and business papers.

He was sometimes accused of being incredibly stingy, but he could be wonderfully generous, too. He sometimes paid a restaurant to organize a party for the entire dance company with which he was touring, and he never allowed a dancer to pay for his or her own restaurant meal. It's true that he expected his wealthy friends to pick up the tab for dinner, but he also repaid them with countless tickets to his performances and invitations to the gala parties afterward.

Perhaps the greatest contrast in him, however, was in how he related to people. Although he was a loner by nature, he almost always surrounded himself with friends and colleagues. For performers, a theater full of appreciative fans is very fulfilling, but the feeling doesn't last. When the curtain falls, a theater can be a lonely and empty place. Even for the self-reliant Rudolf, the joy he derived from dancing and from the admiration of his audiences was not enough; he needed the love and comfort of friends, and indeed developed a keen instinct for true and loyal friendship. The onetime misfit used to say, "Friendship isn't something you get by looking for it. It is something that happens. You have an instinct for knowing who is sincere and who is trying to use you."

In various cities around the world, he carefully selected and made deep friendships, not just with individuals but with whole families. His adopted families, as he called them, provided balance to Rudolf's often lonely, nomadic existence. The Pushkins and the Romankovs in Russia had been the first of these, and he considered the Goslings his adopted parents. As he began to travel to the United States, he made friends with Andre and Natasha Harley in New York City and Armen Bali and her family in San Francisco.

Rudolf's family album. Just a few of the many people who so enriched Rudolf's life. Top row: (left) goddaughter Alexandra Alguire; (right) Alexis Badiyi, the granddaughter of Natasha and Andre Harley. Middle row: (left) Johanna and Caroline Jude; (center) future ballerina Katherine Healy; (right) the Bali family — Arthur, Armen, Jeanette Etheredge and her husband, Bill. Bottom row: (left) King and I *costar Liz Robertson and Michael Alguire; (center) Dillon and Milica Kennedy; (right) Florence and Charles Jude.*

The parents of both the Harleys had been financial supporters of Diaghilev's, and their home was always filled with laughter and brilliant conversation. Eventually Rudolf came to depend on Natasha to host many of his parties in New York. He fondly called Andre and Natasha, and their children, Tatiana and Tamara, his New York family.

Armen Bali owned a restaurant, Bali's, in San Francisco, and she first met Rudolf when she invited him to come to dinner. He felt an immediate bond, and they spoke Russian together until the early morning hours. Not long after, on a return trip from Australia, Rudolf had a long layover in San Francisco. He jumped into a taxi and sped to the restaurant. When he walked in, he asked Bali shyly, "Do you remember me?" She was stunned that such a famous person could even ask such a question. In that instant, he found himself "adopted" by Bali and her two grown children, Arthur Bali and Jeanette Etheredge. Now Rudolf had a San Francisco family.

Through the years, other families were added in cities around the world, including the Judes in Paris, the Hubners in Vienna, the Pignottis in Milan, and my family in Toronto. Rudolf especially enjoyed being around the children of these families and observing their comings and goings. All of us have stories about him spending hours playing on the floor with our children or offering fatherly advice. His close friend Tessa Kennedy remembers the very specific advice he gave two of her teenagers. To one son, who wanted to become an actor, he counseled, "Learn the plays and sonnets of Shakespeare. When you can roll your tongue around the iambic pentameter verses, then you can act." That son was the future movie star Cary Elwes. To her budding painter, Damian, he advised, "Read *The Romantic Agony*. You will never be able to paint from your heart until you understand this book."

Rudolf was often asked if he regretted not having children of his own. Although there was a part of him that missed the experience, his answer was always the same. "I would be a terrible father. They could never have normal home life. It is a terrible pressure for children of famous people to live up to their famous parent. No, I think children deserve better than father who is always gone on a tour."

Rudolf's nomadic existence meant that he didn't have much of a home base, but nevertheless he purchased properties in New York City, Paris, London, Monte Carlo, and on the Caribbean island of St. Barts. He also owned a sprawling farm in the Virginia countryside and a group of three tiny islands called Li Galli off the coast of Italy in the Mediterranean. His talent, hard work, and fame had enabled him to amass a fortune, and he made up for the dreary cramped rooms of his childhood by spending lavishly on these homes and their furnishings.

An invitation to dine with Rudolf at any of his homes was something to treasure. Splendid meals were served, the best wines flowed, and conversation was lively and intelligent. Your dinner companions could include writers, filmmakers, artists, business people, musicians, and of course, dancers. Depending on the guests, the conversation could jump from Russian to English to French, Italian, or German. Rudolf could converse in them all, as well as in a little remembered Tatar.

Each one of his many homes seemed to suit a different mood. His apartments in New York's Dakota building and on Paris' Quay Voltaire, for example, reflected the sensual dancer. They were as sumptuous as the stage settings for one of his ballets. He used dark, warm earth tones and draped the furniture and windows with the rare, exotic fabrics that he so enjoyed collecting. He also collected precious oil paintings, maps and old lithographs, Oriental carpets, and rare musical instruments.

The Virginia farmhouse, by contrast, was sparsely furnished — there was not even a dining-room table — but it contained everything Rudolf considered essential for a home: a mountain of books, videotapes, and records; musical instruments (in this case, keyboards and a church organ

Rudolf always enjoyed performing with children. Here he is seen as Drosselmeyer in his own production of The Nutcracker, *as the King in Rodgers and Hammerstein's* The King and I *in Toronto, and as Prince Myshkin with the Berlin Opera Ballet in Valery Panov's* The Idiot.

so big that it filled an entire room); and enough beds to sleep an army of guests. Huge trees lined and canopied the long drive leading up to the plantation-style house, and Rudolf was thrilled by the sight of deer leaping across his property. With its open fields, shaded woods, and clear streams, the farm offered Rudolf a safe haven of natural beauty.

His oceanside homes in St. Barts and Li Galli did not overlook sandy beaches or calm, pastel seas. He preferred the power, menace, and drama of waves crashing on rocks. Some of his guests complained that the noise of the churning ocean kept them awake, but for Rudolf, the rhythm of the waves made him sleep soundly.

Of all the properties he owned, the one that seemed to hold the most romance for Rudolf was the historic Li Galli, three rocky islands off the coast of Positano, Italy. Rudolf bought Li Galli from the family of Leonide Massine, who had been a legendary dancer himself and was one of the most important choreographers of Diaghilev's Ballets Russes. According to local legend, Li Galli were three of the Siren islands mentioned in Homer's *Odyssey*. In that epic poem, mythological sea nymphs with haunting, beautiful voices lure passing sailors to their deaths on the rocky shores beneath them. To save himself and his shipmates from the Sirens' calls, Odysseus plugs the crew members' ears with wax and instructs them to tie him to the ship's mast before they sail past the islands. He was determined both to make it through and to hear the Sirens' enchanting song.

Rudolf took great pride in his islands' history. He would perch high on the rocky cliffs, often playing a portable keyboard, while he looked out across the shining sea. He told his friends that when he died, he wished to be buried at Li Galli.

Although Rudolf loved all his properties, not one of them replaced his love for the stage. Indeed, he never let anything, whether it was a fear of flying or a desire for a comfortable life, stand in the way of his dancing. The Tatar nomad followed his lust for travel to small towns and world capitals, and throughout his career he performed in more places, to more audiences, in more ballets, with more dance companies, than anyone else in history. When he was asked where his home base was, he answered, "For me, I put down roots on the stages of world. My roots are my work. The stage is my home."

9

THE GATECRASHER

From childhood, I gatecrashed doors of opportunity.
— Rudolf Nureyev

Although Rudolf had all the success he could have desired, he was always looking for new challenges and opportunities. Naturally, the public saw him only as a ballet dancer, but Rudolf never allowed himself to be limited by the expectations of others. He wanted to try his hand at other art forms. Not surprisingly, his twin passions for music and movement led him to choreography.

The first full-length ballet he created, in 1964, was *Raymonda,* based on Marius Petipa's last great ballet for the Maryinsky. Unfortunately, a dark shadow hung over the Royal Ballet's premiere. While the production was in rehearsal, Margot Fonteyn received the horrific news that her husband, Tito Arias, had been gunned down at close range in Panama. He would end up permanently paralyzed. Shortly before opening night, Arias suffered a relapse, and Fonteyn rushed to his bedside. The ballerina had to be replaced for the premiere.

By all recorded accounts, neither the opening night nor the choreography was successful. The steps Rudolf had created were too complicated — a criticism that would follow him throughout his choreographic career.

Rudolf in Murray Louis's Moment. *"I did not come to the West to make a big career or to achieve status. I came because I was interested in dancing everything."*

Even the Goslings, writing as Alexander Bland, reported, "[*Raymonda*] showed more promise than achievement." The Royal Ballet quickly dropped it from its repertoire, but Rudolf would rework and revive the ballet for other companies during the course of his career.

Though still a newcomer to choreography, Rudolf next tackled the much-loved *Swan Lake* for the Vienna State Opera. Traditionally, the ballet had focused on the female leads — the White Swan Queen, Odette, and the Black Swan, Odile. In Rudolf's production, the focus was on Prince Siegfried. This time, he scored a tremendous success.

Rudolf would go on to mount many ballets — classical as well as original pieces, such as his *Tancredi* and *Manfred*. He showed much intelligence in his reconstructions of the classical ballets, but the interpretations were often daring and therefore controversial. Before he choreographed any ballet, he did exhaustive research into its music, decor, and history. He told the *New York Times* dance critic Anna Kisselgoff, "If you have an idea that eats you up, you just can't do something, you have to do something that doesn't let you sleep!" Despite his enthusiasm and his hard work, Rudolf was considered by critics a greater dancer than he was a choreographer.

Every time he ventured into new artistic spheres, Rudolf said he was made to feel like a gatecrasher. In fact, in an interview with the *New York Times* dance writer John Gruen, Rudolf asserted that he'd felt that way his whole life. "From childhood," he said, "I gatecrashed doors of opportunity, beginning with Kirov School."

Rudolf even saw his defection to the West as a form of gatecrashing. He often said he had defected not only for his personal freedom, but also to expand his artistic horizons. In the magazine *After Dark*, he said, "The whole point for me was to feed on a new dance vocabulary, a new way of thinking, a new structure — something that would be very different from classical ballet. I did not come to the West to make a big career or to achieve status. I came because I was interested in dancing everything.

What goaded me was the fact that if I didn't try everything, then my life would be wasted."

By the late 1960s, Rudolf had already worked with several of the greatest European contemporary choreographers, including Kenneth MacMillan, Roland Petit, and Rudi van Dantzig. But he wanted to push into what was unexplored territory for him — American modern dance.

Until the early 1970s, ballet and modern dance stayed firmly in their own camps. This was partly because they had such different roots. Ballet grew out of the stately fifteenth- and sixteenth-century court dances of Italy and France, while modern dance was a twentieth-century creation that drew its inspiration from the more earthly dances of the Orient, Greece, and Africa. The technique required for both is also different. Classical ballet is a formal art based on the five turned-out positions of the feet, and it emphasizes extreme precision and unnatural body posture. The dancers move through set patterns on the stage, striving to defy gravity and create an effect of otherworldly grace. Modern dancers, on the other hand, rebelled against the formality of ballet technique, performing in bare feet and with uninhibited movements. Modern dancemakers experimented with new ways to move their bodies, often using opposing energies such as contraction and release. Even the themes explored by the two dance forms were different. Although both borrowed from legends and ancient myths, classical ballets were often based on storybooks, while modern dance generally investigated human psychology and emotions.

Today, ballet dancers welcome the chance to perform modern dance, but in the 1970s the two distinct camps tended to be more like warring tribes. As a result, Rudolf had a hard time coaxing modern American choreographers to work with him. But he persisted, and eventually led the way to peace between the two camps. His willingness to experiment

Always on the lookout for new challenges and opportunities, and eager to spread his wings beyond the world of ballet, Rudolf worked with many modern and contemporary choreographers. Here he is seen in José Limón's Moor's Pavane *(the author and Mary Jaso are in the background),* Martha Graham's Appalachian Spring, *and Glen Tetley's* Pierrot Lunaire.

inspired other ballet dancers to follow him, and modern choreographers became more open to working with classical ballet companies. When reviewing the accomplishments of Rudolf Nureyev, history may record his brave, pioneering efforts to bring together ballet and American modern dance as one of his greatest achievements.

In 1971, after years of trying, Rudolf convinced the choreographer Paul Taylor to work with him. Eventually, Murray Louis, José Limón, and Martha Graham also gave in to Rudolf's persuasion. Murray Louis admitted that he had been reluctant to work with Rudolf, but said that after seeing him dance in the film version of *Don Quixote*, he realized they had much in common: "Lust for moving, determination, chutzpah, vigor, and audacity . . ." Rudolf would dance three of Louis's pieces, *Vivace*, *The Canarsie Venus*, and *Moment*. For Louis, it was a happy collaboration. "Rudolf was an absolute dynamo and to hook onto his engine and go with it was fabulous."

Martha Graham, the aged high priestess of modern dance, finally agreed to work with Rudolf in 1975, but she insisted that he must train first in her particular technique. Rudolf was so eager to collaborate with her that he humbly bowed to her demands. He was willing to make every sacrifice in order to learn from her. Eventually, he danced several of her pieces, including *Night Journey*, *Appalachian Spring*, and *El Penitente.* The most exciting works, however, were the two dance pieces she created specially for him: *Lucifer* and *The Scarlet Letter.*

For Rudolf, these were fruitful partnerships. Forcing his classically trained body to move in the very different styles of modern dance was difficult, but he loved the new language of steps. He threw himself into each new piece of choreography, licking his lips and saying, "Steps make my mouth water!"

Often Rudolf waived his superstar salary, even taking no money at all, just so he could work with a choreographer who interested him. At the time, many modern companies were desperate for financial help, and his sold-out performances brought a much-needed windfall. For Martha Graham's opening night of *Lucifer*, some tickets sold for ten thousand dollars each.

By including the works of modern choreographers in his Nureyev and Friends tours, he brought them to a wider audience. He had created Nureyev and Friends in 1974, realizing a great dream of forming a company of his own. This group became part of the international dance scene, and provided Rudolf with the opportunity to satisfy his obsession for performing. Gathering dancers from various companies and choosing repertoire from a wide range of styles, he organized worldwide tours. These marathon excursions required versatility and stamina, because he often danced every single ballet, and therefore several different styles, in one evening. The group also set a precedent that other popular artists have since copied by creating their own "Friends" performances.

Despite Rudolf's heavy dancing schedule during the 1970s and 1980s, he managed to find time to appear in two motion pictures. Because of his popularity and his charismatic appearance, it was inevitable that Rudolf would be approached to appear on screen. He loved the movies and could not resist the opportunity. However, both *Valentino* (1977) and *Exposed* (1983) were box-office duds. When reporters asked him if he had made a mistake in trying to become an actor, he shrugged his shoulders and smiled. "Let's be honest," he admitted. "I gatecrashed. But everyone would like the chance to be a movie star!"

The films that record Rudolf's dance performances were far more successful. Seventeen films capture his appearances in full-length ballets and several dozen shorter films record him performing other works. The most highly regarded was a film of his own production of *Don Quixote* with the Australian Ballet. He danced the lead, directed the film, and supervised its editing. It is still considered by many to be the best film ever made of a ballet.

Wallace Potts, a filmmaker and close friend of Rudolf's, was the assistant director of *Don Quixote*. He thought Rudolf was a natural film-maker. "He had in his own mind how ballet footage should be shot and, in both *Don Quixote* and later in his *Nutcracker*, performed by the Paris Opéra, Rudolf had nearly all the camera shots mapped out in his head before he started shooting," Potts explained. "He insisted on shooting with close-ups, moving camera shots, and crane shots, like the techniques used in filming a Hollywood musical. This had never been done before for ballet films, and it made ballet film more exciting."

These movies, along with his appearances on television variety shows and in documentaries, presented him to millions of people who other-wise would never have had a chance to see him dance. One of Rudolf's most famous television appearances was on "The Muppet Show." The Muppets' creator, Jim Henson, invited him to star with Kermit the Frog and his "biggest" leading lady, Miss Piggy. Rudolf performed a couple of song-and-dance numbers, as well as a comic duet, *Swine Lake*, with another pig (the Royal Ballet's Graham Fletcher inside a pig costume). The dance ended up as a hilarious battle instead of a loving pas de deux.

These years of moving from company to company and of venturing into the artistic mediums of others only deepened Rudolf's sense that he was an outsider. He did say, however, that there was one company that always made him feel truly at home – the National Ballet of Canada. "I was lucky in Toronto," he told the *Globe and Mail*'s dance critic, Deirdre Kelly. "I have nice relationships there, and never again I came across that. No other company . . . is of same warmth as Canadians. In National Ballet, I was *not* a gatecrasher."

Rudolf came to the National Ballet in August 1972 to mount his own

One of Rudolf's most memorable — and most enjoyable — appearances was with Kermit and Miss Piggy on "The Muppet Show."

version of *Sleeping Beauty* and to begin a series of long North American tours. The company had been founded twenty-one years earlier by Celia Franca. Like Ninette de Valois before her, Franca knew that Rudolf had much to offer her company; for his part, he was impressed by her beautifully trained dancers.

None of us will forget the afternoon he arrived. It was the last half hour of a long day and the rehearsal was in chaos; we were all endeavoring to learn the tangle of choreography that was the ballet's finale. Ever so slowly, silence crept across the large studio, from one person to the next. Tension gripped the air. All eyes eventually turned to the figure in the doorway. Rudolf Nureyev had entered the studio.

He had come straight from the airport to take a look at how things were going. After a brief hello, he sat down and, in his usual business-like manner, encouraged us to go back to work. Even in repose, he was so charismatic that it was impossible to ignore his presence.

At thirty-four, Rudolf was at the stage in his career when no one could think about ballet without thinking of his name. The entire company was excited about performing with this superstar, but we were also nervous about working with a man whose temper was as legendary as his dancing.

Our first few days with Rudolf went smoothly. We had braced ourselves for a few outbursts, but mercifully none appeared. He was surprised, I think, by how friendly we were to each other and to him. Not at all sure that this family atmosphere, as he called it, was sincere, he teased us and called our friendliness provincial. But most people, even loners, want to be accepted and liked, and Rudolf proved to be no different.

As the weeks, months, and years of successful collaboration passed, a strong, loving relationship developed between the superstar and our company. Of course, he was a serious taskmaster, and as he did everywhere, he often shouted corrections at us in rehearsals or from the wings. But he sometimes softened his commands by adding, "Now, do as Papa says!" To the press he talked about "my" Canadian dancers, or about "my protégés," even though he was not our artistic director. He made many opportunities for several members of the company, particularly for our two youngest stars, Karen Kain and Frank Augustyn. He invited Kain to dance with him in several other companies, and he bragged to anyone who would listen that "Frank's Bluebird is the best in the West."

Rudolf appreciated excellence in all forms, and one less public figure who caught his attention was Susanne Menck, the National Ballet's staff choreologist. A choreologist uses a special notation system, much like music notes, to record ballets, preserve choreography, and help restage dance works. Rudolf cast the tall, regal Menck as the Queen in *Sleeping*

The fairy scene from Rudolf's production of Sleeping Beauty *with the National Ballet of Canada. The wicked fairy, Carabosse, and her monsters are surrounded by the King and Queen, their court, and the fairies.*

Beauty. When she was not onstage, she continued the painstaking work of recording the ballet's score with the Benesh Notation system. Three long years later, she finally finished the monumental undertaking, and she presented Rudolf with one of the scorebooks. He was overcome, calling it a work of art and showing it off to many friends and colleagues.

By his mere presence, Rudolf had a way of lifting our spirits and making our lives, both on the stage and off, more exciting and interesting. The electricity with which he danced was contagious, and we too danced with more spark. Sometimes, it was a few of his well-chosen words that emboldened us. Before our very first performance at the Metropolitan Opera House in New York, for instance, he gathered us together onstage as the orchestra warmed up. We were about to perform his *Sleeping Beauty*, and we were very anxious. He spoke quietly. "There is no need for you to be nervous. You would not be here if I did not think you would astound audience and critics. You will overwhelm them with your beauty and purity of style. More important, tonight *you, yourselves,* will discover just how good you really are!"

True to his prediction, the company did score a success and attain new prominence. And we dancers developed a new confidence in ourselves and a loyalty to Rudolf that lasts to this day.

By the end of the 1970s, Rudolf had taken on the dance world and conquered it. But he was past forty, an age by which most dancers have retired. In every single interview, he was asked the same question: "When do you plan to stop dancing?" He borrowed the reply Margot Fonteyn had given some years earlier, when she was asked the same tiresome query: "I'll stop when the audience no longer wants to see me."

For Rudolf, it was a safe reply. His audiences simply were not yet ready to stay away from the dancer they had come to worship.

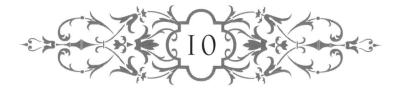

10

DANCING HOME

Ballet, even in Russia, would not be what it is today without him.
— Anna Kisselgoff

By 1981, Rudolf had been in the West for twenty years. As one writer put it, he was not just a star in the ballet, but a force. By that time, many of the male dancers who had risen to fame in the golden age were becoming artistic directors. Eric Bruhn became the director of the National Ballet of Canada, Anthony Dowell of the Royal Ballet, Mikhail Baryshnikov of American Ballet Theatre, and Peter Martins of the New York City Ballet. When the Paris Opéra Ballet invited Rudolf to become its new artistic director, he gladly accepted the offer.

The Paris Opéra Ballet is the world's oldest ballet company. Since 1661, when Louis XIV founded the Académie Royale de Danse, many of ballet's greatest choreographers, teachers, and dancers have been associated with the company. Until the nineteenth century, when Russia became ballet's capital, Paris was the center of dance. *La Sylphide, Giselle,* and *Coppélia* are just a few of the many ballets that premiered there.

When the dance world first learned that Rudolf was going to be the director of the Paris company, he seemed not only the perfect choice, but also the only choice. The company was famous for burning out its

Taking a bow with Charles Jude after a performance of Songs of a Wayfarer. *They danced this duet together so often that Rudolf teased Fonteyn by saying, "After you, Charles is my favorite partner."*

directors, and its reputation had begun to slip. Violette Verdy, a beautiful French ballerina who had also been a director, said, "If anyone can do it [revive the company], Nureyev will be the one. He is made of iron." Erik Bruhn agreed. "I think he is the only person in the world who can cut through the terrible red tape." He called Rudolf after his first day as director and asked him how it had gone. "Just fine," Rudolf said, laughing. "I only got angry three times."

Rudolf was full of enthusiasm for his new job. "I have so many beautiful dancers," he would say, "and, like paintings, I must find beautiful frames to put around them." His first step was to bring in new, exciting choreographers and teachers. He mixed the most avant-garde works with ballets by the choreographers who, at that time in his life, most inspired him — including John Neumeier, Rudi van Dantzig, and Glen Tetley. He also added to the repertoire more established works from such dancemakers as George Balanchine and Anthony Tudor, as well as creating several original ballets.

Even with the demands of his directorship, Rudolf continued to dance and to partner other dancers. Although the ballet world is full of rivalries and jealousies, he was confidant enough in his own abilities that rather than be jealous of others, he rejoiced in their talent. When the Soviet dancer Mikhail "Misha" Baryshnikov defected in Toronto in 1974, Rudolf was thrilled that the extraordinary dancer would have a chance at freedom. As soon as he could, Rudolf took Baryshnikov to dinner. He counseled him on how to best handle a career in the West, and he told him about various teachers and companies. But the most important piece of advice he gave was how to avoid being kidnapped by members of the KGB, who were furious that another Soviet star had escaped. "Make sure you stay on front pages of press. It does not matter if it is good publicity or bad — being in the public's eye will be your best safeguard."

Then, pointing to Baryshnikov, who was ten years younger than he was, Rudolf told the rest of us at the table, "Now I will have to work

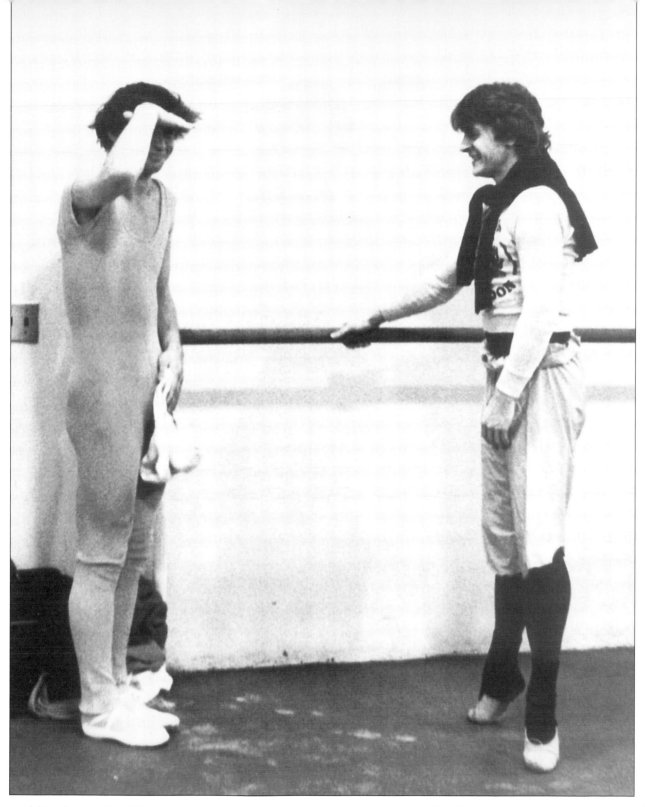

Rudolf embarrassed and Misha Baryshnikov laughing as the rest of the class sings to Rudolf on his thirty-ninth birthday.

ten times as hard to keep up with new competition." Someone asked, "How can you work harder? No one works harder than you!" Rudolf narrowed his eyes and grinned. "Watch me," he said.

To the end of his days, he enjoyed being challenged by younger dancers, particularly those at the Paris Opéra Ballet. He gave such talents as Charles Jude, Laurent Hilaire, Manuel Legris, Sylvie Guillem, and Isabelle Guérin many roles, and he even coached them himself, taking his place in the line of ballet masters that stretched back to the 1600s. He was twenty years older than many of them, just as Margot Fonteyn had been when he danced with her. But he was philosophical about that, and would often tease, "I was dancing full-length ballets when you were still in diapers."

He especially loved dancing with Charles Jude. They performed several ballets together, but many considered their best duet to be *Songs of a Wayfarer*. The most unforgettable moment of *Songs of a Wayfarer* was its ending. Rudolf, the Wayfarer, would stand in a bright spotlight on center stage, staring out into the audience. As the music faded, Jude, the Fate figure, would approach Rudolf from behind and gently take his hand. He would then draw the reluctant Wayfarer toward the back of the stage, out of the spotlight and into the black unknown. As the two figures slowly disappeared into the shadows, Rudolf would turn toward the audience for one last, wistful look. After a still moment of quiet desperation, he would turn back to Jude and allow himself to be led to his fate.

Wayfarer became one of Rudolf's best-known pieces. To many, it seemed to sum up his life: he would never leave the spotlight of his own free will.

In May 1984, the Metropolitan Opera House in New York celebrated its one-hundredth anniversary with a gala evening of song and dance. The program brought together performers from the Met's past and present, and it included popular singers like Lionel Ritchie and John Denver, who were both making their Met debuts.

When Rudolf described the evening to me, it was obvious that it filled him with bittersweet memories. He was not a man to dwell on the past. He often insisted, "I do not look back, just to future." But watching John Denver's excitement as he sang for the first time in the prestigious opera house — and seeing that his mother was there to share it with him — made Rudolf feel sentimental. "Never before I had that. Never have I had pleasure of my mother in audience for first Covent Garden performance, first night at Paris Opéra, first night at Metropolitan Opera House. I stood in wings, wondering if he knew how fortunate he was."

Since his defection, Rudolf had never stopped regretting the pain he had caused his mother. And he'd never stopped missing her. He told the *London Daily Mail*, "It is one of the greatest disappointments in my life that I cannot see my mother. I do not think I will see her again. I have tried many times to convince authorities that it is only humane to allow a mother to be with her son."

In all his years in the West, Rudolf had never publicly criticized the policies of the Soviet Union. He was careful to say that he had left his homeland for artistic reasons alone. He hoped that his relative silence would be interpreted positively by the Soviet authorities, and that in return they would allow his aging and now widowed mother to join him in the West. But nothing seemed to move the hearts of the Soviets.

Rudolf appealed to his fans for help. They set up international committees that began collecting signatures on petitions to send to the Soviet government, pleading that the dancer be allowed to bring his mother to the West. At the same time, Rudolf wrote an open letter to the *New York Times*. In it, he implored the Soviet government to let his mother and his sister Rosa join him. He also appealed personally to Prime Minister Harold Wilson of Britain and to President Jimmy Carter.

Despite all his high-powered allies, it took more than a decade to secure a successful result. In November 1987, the Soviets finally relented

Walking in Ufa during his visit home to see his mother. During this trip, he was asked if he would like to dance again in Russia. He replied thoughtfully, "Whatever is left in me of dancing, I would like to show them." Two years later, the unimaginable happened: the Kirov Ballet invited him to dance in Leningrad.

somewhat. They would not go as far as to let Farida out of the country, but they gave Rudolf a forty-eight-hour visa to journey home. He arrived in Ufa anxious but full of hope.

Tragically, as he described it to me, "The trip was a disaster." Ever since leaving Russia, Rudolf had sent money and gifts to his family through friends. But he was horrified by the conditions in which he found them. His mother, Farida, shared her tiny apartment with her daughter Lilya and her granddaughter Alfiya. Old age and a stroke had left Farida bedridden. She was nearly blind and could speak only in a faint whisper. Worse, her memory was failing. Lilya, injured in a hit-and-run accident, was also an invalid. Alfiya was left to care for her infirm mother and grandmother, as well as be a wife and mother to her husband and child, who also lived in the two-room flat.

With Alfiya and his sister Razida, Rudolf entered his mother's room and bent to kiss her. She whispered to Alfiya, "Is he real or not?" "Yes, it is your son, Rudolf," Alfiya replied. Rudolf had hoped to ask his mother many questions about his birth, his childhood, and his family history. Now it was too late. She was confused and weak, and Rudolf thought that she had not recognized him. Cruelly, the Soviets had waited until Farida was too ill to appreciate that her son had returned. All the years of waiting, all the years of pleading with the government, had ended like this. "They [the Soviet government] are masters of torture. They delivered last blow . . ." said Rudolf bitterly. He left Ufa with an aching heart. His mother died three months later.

The following spring, Rudolf turned fifty years old. In honor of the milestone, Jane Hermann, the presentations director of the Metropolitan Opera House, invited Rudolf's Paris Opéra Ballet to perform for the summer season. She also organized a gala birthday celebration. Rudolf danced with Charles Jude in *Songs of a Wayfarer* and the great opera star Jessye Norman sang the ballet's Gustav Mahler songs. The evening closed with a ceremonial procession called the Grand Défilé. It was the first time that this procession, which is used by the Paris Opéra to mark special occasions, had ever taken place outside of that city.

The procession began with the dramatic strains of Hector Berlioz's "March of the Trojans" filling the vast theater. One hundred students from the Paris Opéra Ballet School, brought to New York specially for the occasion, led the procession. In rising order of rank, the dancers of the Paris Opéra followed the students onto the stage. The stately parade continued with the dance world's directors and choreographers, Rudolf's

Rudolf's fiftieth birthday celebration at the Met. He is surrounded by the dancers of the Paris Opéra Ballet and some of the world's greatest dancers, choreographers, and artistic directors.

partners from the past to the present, and finally, Rudolf's "partner in legend" – Margot Fonteyn.

Following that special evening, for which the ballet world had turned out in full force, Anna Kisselgoff wrote, "Ballet, even in Russia, would not be what it is today without him. Dancer, ballet producer, company director, inspirational model, irresistible force and irritant, catalyst, and galvanizer, Rudolf Nureyev remains a point of reference. . . . This was the Nureyev who raised the standard of dancing throughout the world through his own example."

Time is cruel to dancers. Years of working the body mercilessly, along with the natural effects of aging, can erase a ballet career long before the dancer's heart is ready to leave the stage. Like the Wayfarer, Rudolf, at fifty, was not about to abandon the spotlight.

When the ballet invitations grew more scarce, he looked for other ways to continue performing. In 1989, he was asked to play the role of the King in *The King and I*, a musical based on the true story of a former king of Siam and the English woman he hired to teach in his palace school. Having always admired American musical theater, Rudolf harbored a secret longing to try it himself. He was given a good director and coach to help with his speaking and singing voice, though he joked, "They are rearranging my croaking." He was also pleased to have as his costar Liz Robertson, whom he admired.

While preparing for the opening in Toronto, even Rudolf noted the similarities between the character he played and himself. "King is like me, he loves absolute power and control. He has burning desire to learn everything. He is obsessed for knowledge." Rudolf possessed the presence, manner, and look of an Asian ruler, and like the king of Siam, he was accustomed to having people adore and worship him like a god.

Unfortunately for Rudolf, not all the critics adored him, and the reviews for *The King and I* were mixed. Some thought he was perfect for the part, but others felt he should stick to dancing. The criticism left him unfazed, however, and he viewed the experience in the same way he had his brief sojourn into motion pictures. "So, yet again, I am accused of being intruder or gatecrasher. But audiences enjoyed show, I enjoyed playing in show, and I learned in the process of doing it. I do not allow praise or criticism of others to dictate what I do."

By 1989, Rudolf's life was changing and so was the world around him. That November, in a dramatic turn of events, two Cold War barriers

Venturing into new territory as the King in
The King and I, *1989.*

came crashing down. The first was the hated Berlin Wall, which had been erected in August 1961, only two and a half months after Rudolf's defection. For twenty-eight years, the wall had divided the city of Berlin, and it stood as both a real and a symbolic barricade for people trapped behind the Iron Curtain. But at long last the Cold War was over, the wall came down, and one country after another in the old Soviet bloc shed its Communist government.

In the same month, another barrier — one that was not as internationally significant, but that nevertheless had been a powerful symbol — came down. Rudolf Nureyev, arguably Russia's most famous defector, was invited to dance with the Kirov Ballet. The ban against Rudolf's dancing in Russia had, like the Berlin Wall, lasted twenty-eight years.

Newspapers around the world heralded the invitation as an example of improved relations between West and East. Common sense, however, told Rudolf that he should not accept. He was too old. The young dancer who had so dazzled Leningrad in the 1950s no longer existed. In the end, though, he simply couldn't resist.

A television crew accompanied Rudolf and was to capture the event for "Sunday Morning with Charles Kuralt," in a segment called "Dancing Home." Unfortunately, he arrived in Leningrad with one injured foot. Then, during rehearsals, he injured the other one. Grimly, he joked, "I was left with no foot to stand on! But I am from school of Margot Fonteyn. You do not cancel unless you are near death!"

On November 17, Rudolf prepared to dance again in the theater he had once referred to as "that most sacred shrine." In the audience to welcome him home were several of his partners from his Kirov days, including Natalia Dudinskaya, Irina Kolpakova, and Ninel Kurgapkina; his old friends Tamara Zakrzhevskaya and Liuba and Leonid Romankov; his sister Razida and his niece Alfiya; and countless former fans. Seated in a box was Anna Udeltsova, his first ballet teacher. She was one hundred years old. Though she was happy to watch him dance one last time, she exclaimed, "I had to live to one hundred to see him!"

Unfortunately, his performance did not go well. Rudolf sensed that the audience was applauding for the dancer he had been, not the dancer he was — an injured fifty-one-year-old man. He was deeply disappointed by his own performance, but nevertheless regarded the invitation as a personal victory. He said, "I had to wait almost thirty years. I feel vindicated."

Although the performance was discouraging, the journey gave him the chance to see and talk freely with many of his old colleagues, friends, and family members. Rudolf also visited his former ballet school. After his defection, every trace of his Kirov career had been erased. Photos and references to him were cut out of books, films of his dancing were removed from sight, and his name was eliminated from the school's list of graduates. It was as if he had never existed. Finally, in a gesture meant to honor his return, pictures of him were hung in the school's museum.

For Rudolf, "dancing home" had proved to be bittersweet.

II

FİNALE

I will dance to the last drop of blood.
— Rudolf Nureyev

The year of Rudolf's journey home to Leningrad, an angry contract dispute ended his association with the Paris Opéra Ballet. Despite the hurt feelings surrounding his leaving, he was proud of what he had accomplished there. Under his direction, the company had regained its lost glory. He had increased the repertoire, elevated the standard of the dancing, advanced the careers of many young dancers, and toured the company abroad. He had even added badly needed rehearsal space in the dome of the theater. After his death, that space would be named Espace Nureyev in his honor.

Time was now running out for Rudolf, but still he could not bear to leave the stage. He admitted, "I am driven by my own demons." He accepted invitations to dance in smaller and smaller auditoriums. Soon, the man who had once danced in the world's greatest theaters, accompanied by the finest musicians, was dancing to tape recordings.

Why did he refuse to stop? The simple answer is that he could not face life without dance or the stage. He was not dancing for the critics at the beginning of his career, when they had struggled to find enough words with

His last appearance at the Met, May 6, 1992. He is conducting Romeo and Juliet *for American Ballet Theatre a mere six weeks after a brush with death.*

which to praise him. And he was not dancing for them now, when they were searching for new ways to say he was past his prime. He had never danced for the approval of anyone. He danced because he simply loved dancing.

But it was clear to everyone, including Rudolf, that he could not go on much longer. Charles Jude, who toured with him at this stage of his career, said that Rudolf danced the full-length classical ballets beyond the age of most male dancers because those ballets forced him to work harder and with more precision, thereby maintaining his technique.

Nevertheless, relentless interviewers continued to ask what Rudolf called his Hiroshima question: "When will you stop dancing, Mr. Nureyev?" Sometimes he joked, "It is state secret. I am not divulging! It is classified information!" But more often, he replied defiantly, "For me, dance and life are one. I will dance to the last drop of blood."

Occasionally, someone created a work that suited his talent as a mature artist. The former Danish ballet star Flemming Flindt, for example, choreographed *The Overcoat,* a ballet based on a short story by Nikolai Gogol. Cleverly, Flindt created a role that demanded more of Rudolf as an actor than as a dancer. In so doing, both he and Rudolf earned great praise from the critics.

When Rudolf danced roles that required more from his aging body, however, the critics were unforgiving. They said that his shoulders and back in arabesque looked strained, and that his landings from jumps were leaden. There were even critics who said that he was destroying his own legend. Before his death, however, Erik Bruhn had countered, "Rudolf cannot destroy his legend — it is there for all to see in newsprint, photos, books, and on film. And his dancing is burned in the minds of all who saw him while he created that legend."

For those who chose to see it, he still had artistry to offer. The dance writer Gary Smith wrote, "Of course, the elasticity is gone. Those once mercurial flights into space, hovering at the edge of the universe, are no

An early photo of Rudolf practicing the piano. He had a lifelong love of classical music. When he ended his dancing career, he transformed that passion into a second career as a conductor.

more. But the truth is, those glorious tricks, as dazzling as they were, are only a small measure of the genius that is Nureyev."

By 1990, *The King and I* tours had concluded and his dance schedule had greatly diminished. Retirement was out of the question for a person who believed so strongly in the power of work, so Rudolf decided it was time to pursue his one last dream — becoming a conductor.

Among other things, conducting would partly fulfill his desperate need to remain in the spotlight. It gave him the chance to learn a new skill, to create, and to still feel the surge of music through his body. With his new passion, he could continue to savor the smell of the greasepaint and the roar of the crowd.

From his boyhood, Rudolf had loved music, and over the years he had educated himself thoroughly in classical music. For years, he had thought about conducting, but he had not wanted to sacrifice his dancing. Now that he had the time, however, he sought out the world-famous conductor Leonard Bernstein, his neighbor at the Dakota, for advice. Bernstein thought that conducting was perfect for a person with Rudolf's musicality and keen memory. The dancer had been given similar encouragement by two other famous conductors – Karl Bohm and Herbert von Karajan. Thus inspired, Rudolf, as he had done when he was a young dancer, approached the best teacher he could find to help him get started. He called on his old friend Professor Wilhelm Hubner, who had been the president of the Vienna Philharmonic Orchestra.

Rudolf considered his move to Vienna a good omen, because it had always been a place of firsts and opportunities for him. It had been there, in 1955, that he had performed in the West for the first time, at the World Youth Festival. Later, the Vienna State Opera House had offered him many opportunities as both a choreographer and a dancer. They asked him to mount his first productions of *Swan Lake* and *Don Quixote*, as well as his first original ballet, *Tancredi.* He had even danced his first Balanchine ballet – *Apollo* – there. And it was in Vienna that Margot Fonteyn and Rudolf had received their longest curtain call. When a collection of commemorative stamps was issued to honor the one-hundredth anniversary of the opera house, one of them depicted Fonteyn and Rudolf dancing *Swan Lake*.

Now he was back in Austria, poised on the threshold of a whole new career. Professor "Papa" Hubner was pleased to take the diligent, enthusiastic Rudolf under his wing.

Rudolf's first brave attempt at conducting an orchestra was with a Nureyev and Friends tour on January 28, 1991, in Rockford, Illinois. He chose Rockford because he wanted to take his first steps as a conductor outside the glare of the international spotlight. He conducted excerpts from *Sleeping Beauty* for a performance by his own dancers. Charles Jude remembers, "During rehearsals with the orchestra, he was a little unsure of

This Austrian stamp commemorating the hundredth anniversary of the Vienna State Opera House shows Rudolf and Fonteyn in Swan Lake.

himself, like a child, asking their advice at times about certain musical passages. Before the performance, he was very nervous, but it went very well."

When he returned to Vienna, he continued his lessons with Hubner and also worked with Dr. Franz Moser, the director of the Vienna Residenz Orchestra. Within a few short months, Rudolf stood at the podium in the Palais Auersperg to conduct the orchestra in an evening of Tchaikovsky, Haydn, and Mozart. He dazzled everyone, including the normally hard-to-impress musicians. Soon, he was fielding requests to conduct orchestras all over Europe and reveling in the respect of his musicians, who found him to be a passionate, enthusiastic conductor.

Sadly, he had little time to enjoy his new career, for in the fall of 1991 his health started to fail. Rudolf was in Budapest when he had an attack of kidney stones and had to be rushed back to Vienna for surgery.

In many ways, 1991 had not been an easy year to endure. Along with his own health problems, Rudolf had to face a great loss. Margot

Fonteyn died after a long battle with cancer on February 21, 1991 — the twenty-ninth anniversary of their first performance together in *Giselle.*

Throughout their years together, they had remained the closest of friends. During Fonteyn's illness, Rudolf called her often and visited her whenever he could. Her husband's long-term care and her own battle with cancer had drained her finances, and she spent her last years living modestly on her ranch in Panama. In fact, Rudolf anonymously paid part of her medical bills. When she eventually died, he was relieved that her suffering was over, but he missed her dreadfully. Rudolf told me, "Almost everything I learned about handling career in West, I learned from Margot. I don't know what would have happened to me if I had not found her, maybe big flash and then quick fade. I owe her everything."

Rudolf often said that he owed his development as an artist to Alexander Pushkin, Sir Frederick Ashton, Erik Bruhn, and Margot Fonteyn. Now they were all dead. By 1991, he had also lost his parents; his sister Lilya; his impresario, Sol Hurok; his agent, Sandor Gorlinsky; and his beloved friend and mentor, Nigel Gosling. To overcome his grief for Fonteyn, Rudolf did what he had always done in order to survive. He immersed himself in his work.

One month after his kidney surgery in Vienna, Rudolf not only was back on his feet but also insisted on fulfilling a contract he had signed for a Nureyev and Friends tour of Australia. After that tour, he danced again in Berlin, and then, in Budapest in February 1992, he danced the role of an angel in a ballet about another world traveler, Christopher Columbus. But those audiences did not see the dancer they had remembered. In fact, most came away from those performances bitterly disappointed, believing that he was simply too old to dance. They did not know that he was ill, or that they had just seen Rudolf Nureyev's last performances as a dancer.

Rudolf was suffering from the effects of AIDS. Very few people knew that he had been battling the disease since 1984, when he had learned he was HIV-positive. He had kept going all those years, taking whatever new medical treatments were offered, and never letting up on his demanding work schedule or the pursuit of his goals.

Because he was both a private and a practical man, Rudolf had confided in only a few people about his condition. He knew that if the news of his illness became public, his contract offers could be affected. This was a time when there was tremendous prejudice against people with HIV and AIDS, and some countries, including the United States, barred the entry of persons who were HIV-positive or had full-blown AIDS. But Rudolf also simply did not want people talking about his illness. As always, he wanted all the focus to be on his artistic accomplishments.

Early in 1992, Rudolf was invited to spend a month conducting a local orchestra in the Tatar city of Kazan. Despite his deteriorating condition, he pounced on the opportunity, even though it meant living in poor conditions in the bone-chilling Russian winter. For three weeks, he enjoyed himself, working hard with the orchestra, taking pleasure in the companionship of his fellow Tatar musicians. It was as if his travels had brought him full circle, back to the land of his ancestors. But one frozen night, when he joined the musicians for a trip to a sauna, he caught a chill. The next day, he was ill with a high fever. He was rushed to Leningrad, where he was treated for pneumonia.

Douce François, a close and loyal friend of Rudolf's, had traveled with him to Russia. She became concerned when his health did not improve, and soon she insisted that he return to Paris. He did so, but not before spending his fifty-fourth birthday with his old friends the Romankovs and with his former Kirov partner, Ninel Kurgapkina.

By the time Rudolf arrived in Paris, he was suffering from an inflammation of the membrane of his heart and was close to death. He was rushed into surgery, where his doctor removed a liter of fluid from around his heart. François's insistence that he return to Paris had saved his life. I spoke with him only two days after his surgery. Already he was telling me about his upcoming engagements – his plans to mount *La Bayadère* for the Paris Opéra Ballet and his conducting premiere at the Metropolitan Opera House. His gleeful enthusiasm made it difficult for me to believe that he had almost died.

Only six weeks after his heart surgery, Rudolf flew to New York to appear for the last time at the Metropolitan Opera House – but this time he would not dance. Instead, he would conduct the orchestra for American Ballet Theatre in the full-length ballet *Romeo and Juliet.* The roles of Romeo and Juliet were danced by two of his favorite dancers from Paris, Laurent Hilaire and Sylvie Guillem. Once again, it was his friend Jane Hermann, now the co-artistic director of American Ballet Theatre, who had arranged the special performance. She could not have given Rudolf a more precious gift.

Sergei Prokofiev's music for *Romeo and Juliet* is fiendishly difficult. It is a very long score that demands tremendous energy from a conductor. By this time, Rudolf was very frail. He had to conserve every bit of his strength just to get through the long rehearsals.

On the evening of May 6, 1992, Rudolf stepped up to the podium. A daunting task lay ahead of him. He would need to find the strength to conduct for the musicians in the pit and for the dancers onstage. Miraculously, he did it, and after the final curtain the theater shook with a thunderous ovation. When Rudolf came onto the stage to take his bows, the audience greeted him with a crescendo of cheers. In the orchestra pit, the musicians rose to their feet and applauded to show their respect for a fellow artist. They also raised their hands in a gesture meant to signify that he had been victorious in his effort. He had triumphed.

Pale and exhausted, Rudolf stood in the brilliant spotlight, gazing out at the dark theater. How many times he had danced there! He remembered the glittering evenings when he had partnered Margot Fonteyn, and he thought of the other ballerinas he had danced with. He recalled the times when the fans had showered him with bouquets of flowers, and he remembered the tumultuous applause of audiences gone mad with excitement. Savoring the love and admiration that engulfed him, he stood alone onstage, his arms outstretched to his audience.

Rudolf's energy was slowly slipping away. Even so, there were moments when his iron willpower seemed to conquer his frail body. He was determined to keep working as long as he could stand. In July, he flew to San Francisco to conduct the orchestra of the University of California.

He stayed with his friend Jeanette Etheredge, the daughter of Armen Bali. My husband and I brought our children from Toronto to say their farewells to Uncle Rudolf. At three, Alexandra was now old enough to hold a conversation with him, and she insisted on sitting on his lap whenever they were together. She called him "Uncle Roo-off." Delighted with his new name, he exclaimed, laughing, "I've been called worse!"

Coincidentally, the Kirov Ballet happened to be performing in San Francisco at the same time. Along with dancers from the San Francisco Ballet and the Kirov, we gathered at Etheredge's well-known restaurant, Tosca's, for late-night dinners and conversation. For thirty years, Etheredge and her mother had welcomed dancers and even whole ballet companies into their lives and their restaurants. Their post-performance parties were legendary in the dance world.

Rudolf's appearance went well, but his conducting movements were very guarded. Afterward, at a post-performance dinner party, his spirits were raised when Wayne Eagling, a former Royal Ballet colleague and now the director of the Dutch National Ballet, invited him to come to Holland to conduct *Petrouchka* on New Year's Day, 1993. Invitations like these gave Rudolf the incentive to keep fighting for his life.

Returning to Paris, he was able, with help from Ninel Kurgapkina and coaches from the Paris Opéra Ballet, to finish mounting his full-length production of *La Bayadère.* He had good days and bad, but he would not allow himself to stop working.

Sadly, it soon became clear to his friend and doctor, Michel Canesi, that Rudolf needed constant care. At first, his close friends set up a schedule, leaving their jobs and homes, and taking turns staying with him in his Paris apartment. With Canesi, who often came to see Rudolf twice a day, they worked out a way for the dancer to stay in the comfort of his beautiful apartment, surrounded by those who loved him.

Marika Besobrasova, the director of Monaco's Académie de Danse Classique Princess Grace, was the first to arrive to take care of her dear friend. She had known Rudolf since soon after his defection, and they had shared a long relationship based on mutual respect. Throughout their many years of friendship, she cherished their long talks about ballet technique. "He gave me clear answers to questions that had plagued me for years," she remembered gratefully.

In the weeks leading up to the premiere of *La Bayadère,* the company witnessed the titanic effort Rudolf made to come and direct the rehearsals. Each day that passed left him weaker, but he struggled on. He refused to speak about his condition, just as he had done with the injuries he suffered during his dance career, and his circle of friends honored his wishes by not speaking of it either. It was as if discussing his illness would have been giving in to it. By not discussing it, he did not have to recognize its existence. And if it didn't exist, he hoped to defy it – and death itself. There were times when we thought he just might succeed.

No one knew how much longer Rudolf could hold on to life. As the *Bayadère* premiere approached, friends and colleagues from all over the

After Rudolf's death, Marika Besobrasova brought Soloria to live with her in Monte Carlo. "Eventually, Soloria became a model of obedience and learned to understand several human languages," Besobrasova later declared.

world journeyed to Paris. Everyone wanted to be with him for what was sure to be his final triumph.

As soon as new friends arrived in Paris, they joined the circle of Rudolf's caregivers. Jeanette Etheredge took over his care from Besobrasova. Later, Jane Hermann, Wallace Potts, and others would take their turns. Douce François, who lived in Paris and for years had helped Rudolf with his personal and business affairs, continued to attend to those masses of details in what was often a thankless job. All of those friends were heroic in the tireless care they gave him.

But there was so much to do. No one in the apartment, for instance, was ever sure how many would be joining Rudolf for lunch or dinner, so efforts were made to prepare meals that were flexible enough, and ample enough, to include anyone who was visiting. And there was one more permanent mouth to feed. Rudolf, whose demanding travel schedule had once made it impossible to have a pet, had finally acquired a dog, Soloria. Now that the Tatar nomad's traveling days were over, Soloria was a last gift to himself.

So along with the worries of providing proper care for Rudolf, his friends had to shoulder the difficulties of a large, untrained animal. When Rudolf phoned Etheredge in San Francisco to tell her that he had bought a dog, she told him, "She better speak English by the time I get there, because I don't speak French!" In fact, Soloria did not seem to understand commands in any of the languages spoken in the apartment: English, French, Russian, or Italian.

One day not long after Etheredge had arrived in Paris, she went to call Rudolf for lunch. When she returned to the table, there was no food. Soloria had helped herself. Her nerves frayed, Etheredge told Rudolf, "You have to find a language that dog can understand!" With that, Rudolf shouted something to Soloria in German. The dog looked up in fright and took off. She hid for two hours. Lunch was lost, but to everyone's amusement and relief, a language Soloria understood had been found.

Rudolf named his dog Soloria after Solor, the part he played in *La Bayadère.* The ballet had brought him success after success over the years, both as a dancer and as a producer. He had first danced the role of the heroic warrior in Russia, at the very beginning of his career when life held nothing but promise, and it was as the magnificent Solor that he was introduced to the West in his first performance in Paris with the Kirov. Although he set only the famous last act of *La Bayadère* for the Royal Ballet in 1963, it had been the first ballet he had produced for a company in the West. Now he was producing it again, in a full-length version that would be his final gift to the world.

As the premiere drew nearer, Rudolf spent the days resting in bed, conserving his energy so that he could attend the evening dress rehearsals. A steady stream of friends dropped by to sit with him and bring him news from around the world. His face lit up with each new guest, and he looked forward to his daily visits from Charles Jude and his

October 8, 1992. Rudolf's final gift to the dance world: his full-length version of La Bayadère *with the Paris Opéra Ballet.*

wife, Florence Clerc, who had also been one of his ballerinas with the Paris Opéra. However, it was the arrival of Maude Gosling, now in her eighties, that brought him the most joy and comfort. In his heart, she had remained his adopted mother.

By this point, he was so weak that long conversations with him were impossible. Mainly, we talked and he listened. But he was proud to tell us about the conducting offers he was continuing to receive. He placed great stock in those contract offers. They signified to him that the world had not turned its back even though he was ill.

Ever since his defection to the West, Rudolf had been a symbol of human strength and tenacity. Throughout his career, he had pushed us, his fellow dancers, to be courageous. Now, facing death, he was teaching all those around him the true meaning of the word "courage."

La Bayadère premiered on October 8, 1992. The audience was overflowing with members of Parisian society, as well as with Rudolf's friends and colleagues, who had converged on Paris to be with him. The dancers of the Paris Opéra, and especially the stars of the evening, Isabelle Guérin, Laurent Hilaire, and Elisabeth Platel, seemed to perform only for Rudolf that night. Some of the company's members had had their battles with him when he was their artistic director, but on that night they danced for him with their hearts and souls.

During the performance, Rudolf lay on a divan in a box seat near to the stage. Those of us who had been with him earlier that day did not know where he found the strength to attend the premiere. But Rudolf "Never-off" had rarely canceled a performance — and this was certainly one he would not allow himself to miss.

While the audience applauded for the company at the end of the performance, Rudolf was helped to the backstage wings. He was too weak to walk alone. Luigi Pignotti and his doctor, Michel Canesi, supported him. Then the velvet curtain slowly rose, and Rudolf stood on the stage before a theater full of admirers who knew they were witnessing his last curtain call. Tears streamed down every face in the grand theater. Only Rudolf was dry-eyed. He stood on center stage, supported by Laurent Hilaire and Isabelle Guérin, and accepted the outpouring of love, respect, and honor from an audience thanking him for a lifetime of thrilling beauty.

When the curtain fell for the final time, Rudolf's friends and colleagues gathered around him on the stage as France's minister of culture bestowed on him the country's highest cultural honor — the title of Commander of

Arts and Letters. The next day, when the first photos of his gaunt face appeared in the international press, the rest of the world realized what those of us in the audience had known the night before — the greatest dancer of our time, and maybe of all time, had taken his final bow.

Rudolf died in Notre-Dame du Perpétuel Secours Hospital in Paris on the afternoon of January 6, 1993. According to Dr. Canesi, he had not uttered a single complaint throughout his last months of life. He had fought his failing health, as he had every obstacle in his life, with almost superhuman intensity. "When it seemed that he had less than a month to live, he held on for two months," remembered Canesi. "When we thought there was maybe only a week left, he lived on for two weeks. The day before he died, we were sure this would be his last day — but he lived on. Finally, when we thought death was imminent that morning, Rudolf held on until the afternoon."

Rudolf loved life, and he had squeezed every drop of joy out of it. He had held on to life until the very last moment.

On January 12, Rudolf's family, friends, and colleagues from the worlds of dance, music, theater, film, and art gathered once more. This time it was to bid him farewell.

The night before the funeral, a howling rainstorm had shaken people from their sleep. The thunder crackled and exploded over Paris. The night sky was illuminated by streaks of lightning, and rain pounded on the windows. To those of us who have theatrical blood running in our veins, it seemed as if the gods were crying. The next morning, as we made our way with all the mourners through the still-dark city, a fine gray rain began to fall. Hundreds of fans stood on the wet pavement, waiting in patient silence behind police barricades to pay their last respects.

The service took place in the marble foyer of the Paris Opéra House, the same theater where Rudolf had begun his career in the West, and

January 12, 1993. Charles Jude, Jean Guizerix, Manuel Legris, Wilfried Romoli, Francis Malovik, and Koder Belarbi carrying Rudolf's casket down the Grand Staircase in the foyer of the Paris Opéra House to Mahler's Songs of a Wayfarer.

where he had made his final curtain call just three short months before. The ceremony included readings from the works of his favorite writers: Pushkin, Byron, Michaelangelo, Goethe, and Rimbaud. A chamber orchestra played selections from his beloved Bach, as well as from Tchaikovsky. The foyer of the theater was very chilly, and the formal ceremony itself, although grand, did not completely capture the Rudolf who had blazed through our lives. Not until the six pallbearers, led and chosen by Charles Jude, lifted his coffin to descend the Grand Staircase to the music of *Songs of a Wayfarer* did it seem that this was a funeral for Rudolf the dancer.

It was haunting to see Jude, Rudolf's friend and "second favorite partner," carrying the coffin to the strains of Gustav Mahler. It seemed like yesterday that we had watched the two men dance to that same music. Now, in death as in the *Wayfarer* duet, Charles was leading Rudolf to his fate.

Rudolf's grave site at the Sainte-Geneviève-des-Bois cemetery outside Paris. The monument's designer, Ezio Frigerio, wanted to pay tribute to Rudolf, the Tatar nomad, by creating a traveling trunk covered by an Oriental carpet made entirely of glass mosaic tiles.

As the funeral procession slowly made its way to Sainte-Geneviève-des-Bois Cemetery, the sun finally burst forth. At the cemetery, we filed past Rudolf's grave, deep in our own thoughts and memories. Some mourners threw flowers onto the coffin, but the most moving tribute came when the dancers from the Paris Opéra threw their ballet shoes into the open grave. It was their way of saying that Rudolf had taken a piece of their dancing with him.

Then, under a sunny blue sky, we formed small groups to comfort each other. As I listened to my friends reminisce, it occurred to me that maybe, just maybe, the great storm of the night before had been caused by Rudolf gatecrashing once again . . . this time through the gates of heaven.

GLOSSARY OF BALLET TERMS

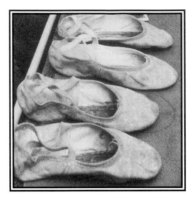

adagio: the class exercises that are practiced to slow music; these exercises are used to develop a dancer's sense of line, grace, and the strength and balance to stand on one leg.

arabesque: a pose in which the dancer stands on one leg while the other is extended to the back; arms and body positions may vary.

barre: a wooden or metal bar that is fastened to a wall and offers a dancer support in the early exercises of a ballet class.

batterie: literally, beats of the leg; a ballet term used to describe the brilliant movements in which the feet and legs beat against each other.

corps de ballet: those members of a company who dance as an ensemble.

double assemblé turns: a double turn in the air with both feet coming together in fifth position; often executed as a series of turns in a circle.

en pointe: the position of the foot in a pointe shoe when the ballerina is standing on the tips of her toes; demi-pointe: the position of the foot when the dancer rises to the ball of the foot; quarter-pointe: the position of the foot when the dancer raises his or her heel off the ground only slightly.

fifth position: in classical ballet, there are five positions of the feet; in fifth position, the legs are crossed and the feet turned out and over-lapped, so that the toe of one foot reaches the heel of the other.

high passé: a position in which the toe of one foot is placed at or above the side of the knee of the supporting leg.

jeté (or grand jeté): a grand jeté is a big leap, usually in a forward direc-tion, with legs in a split position.

pas de deux: literally, a dance for two; in classical ballet, it is a dance usually constructed in three parts: 1) a slow duet danced by a ballerina and her partner; 2) solos performed by both the male and the female dancer; 3) a coda or finale in which both dancers finish their duet together.

pirouette: a turn or multiple spins on one leg; a pirouette can be exe-cuted in many different positions.

plié: the bending of the supporting knee or knees; the plié is an essential movement in ballet that is used in all combinations of steps (i.e., for the takeoffs and landings of jumps and turns); it is one of the first and most important exercises in a ballet class.

port de bras: the carriage or movement of the arms.

Every dancer can trace his roots back to the court of Louis XIV and his Académie Royale de Danse. It is astonishing to discover that, in a direct line of descent from the original academy to the dancers of today, there are so few teachers. From the Académie Royale de Danse, two main branches of training developed: the French-Danish line and the Italian line. Under Marius Petipa, the two lines amalgamated into what became known as the Russian School. Rudolf and his teacher, Alexander Pushkin, were both products of that schooling.

BALLET MASTERS' LEGACY

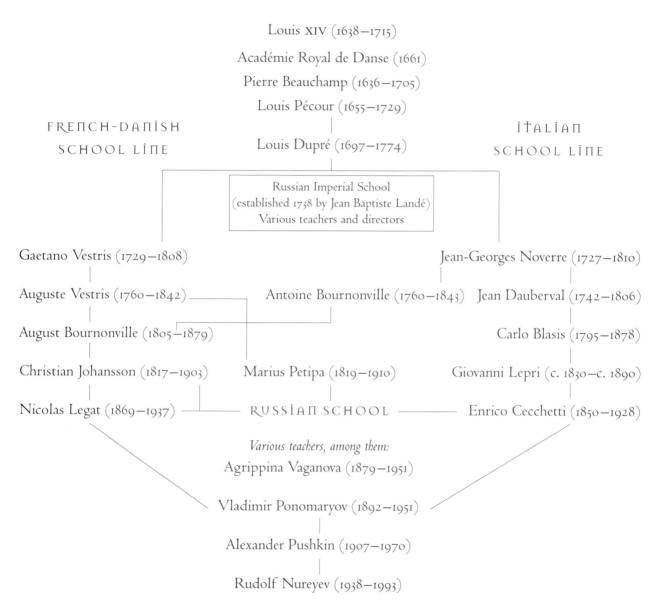

Louis XIV (1638–1715)

Académie Royal de Danse (1661)

Pierre Beauchamp (1636–1705)

Louis Pécour (1655–1729)

FRENCH-DANISH
SCHOOL LINE

Louis Dupré (1697–1774)

ITALIAN
SCHOOL LINE

Russian Imperial School
(established 1738 by Jean Baptiste Landé)
Various teachers and directors

Gaetano Vestris (1729–1808)

Jean-Georges Noverre (1727–1810)

Auguste Vestris (1760–1842)   Antoine Bournonville (1760–1843)   Jean Dauberval (1742–1806)

August Bournonville (1805–1879)

Carlo Blasis (1795–1878)

Christian Johansson (1817–1903)   Marius Petipa (1819–1910)   Giovanni Lepri (c. 1830–c. 1890)

Nicolas Legat (1869–1937)   ——— RUSSIAN SCHOOL ——— Enrico Cecchetti (1850–1928)

Various teachers, among them:
Agrippina Vaganova (1879–1951)

Vladimir Ponomaryov (1892–1951)

Alexander Pushkin (1907–1970)

Rudolf Nureyev (1938–1993)

ACKNOWLEDGMENTS

Publishing a book is like creating a ballet, in that there are so many people behind the scenes whose contributions are essential to the production. It is with gratitude and appreciation that I thank all those who have helped me with their encouragement, guidance, knowledge, and remembrances. I offer particular appreciation and thanks to:

My friends, the respected writers William Stevenson, Monica Jensen-Stevenson, and Dr. Joseph MacInnis, who felt this would be an important book for young artists and talked me into writing it. Their prodding and words of encouragement echoed what Rudolf used to say to me: "If you see something needs to be done, then do it yourself."

Linda McKnight and Bruce Westwood, my literary agents, who from the beginning believed in me and saw the potential in this book. Thank you for your unstinting encouragement, sage advice, and for leading me to the perfect editor and publisher.

Kathy Lowinger, my publisher, who was the first editor to see my manuscript and never gave up on getting it into print. Her own passion for dance helped enormously with the editing. My heartfelt thanks go out to her for her perseverance and masterful guidance.

Avie Bennett, chairman and president of McClelland & Stewart and Tundra, for his support as both a dance patron and a courageous publisher; Sari Ginsberg, for her beautiful design, and the staff of Tundra and McClelland & Stewart for their spirited enthusiasm and superb craftsmanship.

Janice Weaver, my editor, for her expertise and calming guidance.

Lynn Perry, Sandy Perry, Marilyn La Vine, and Bob Gable, who gave me complete access to their personal Nureyev collections and to the research they had assembled for Rudolf during his lifetime. The Marilyn J. La Vine

THE DANCER WHO FLEW

Rudolf Nureyev Collection can be accessed at the Library of Congress in Washington, D.C. It covers the years from 1959 to 1993; includes fifty volumes of newspaper, journal, and magazine writings; and is a complete history of Rudolf's life in ballet.

Wallace Potts, for all his help and advice.

Alfiya Rafikova, Rudolf's niece, for sharing family stories and pictures.

Tamara Zakrzhevskaya, Alexander Storozhuk, the Russian Institute for the History of the Arts, Liuba Romankova-Myasnikova, and Marina Vivien, for their help in Russia.

All the dancers, choreographers, dance writers, and photographers, as well as Rudolf's friends and fans, who have been so generous in sharing their stories about Rudolf and so eager to help me keep his memory alive. One of the best parts of writing this book has been the chance to renew acquaintances, revive friendships, and in some cases even form new ones. My friends, both new and old, include Frank Augustyn, Armen Bali, Clive Barnes, Robert and Virginia Barnett, Mikhail Baryshnikov, Marika Besobrasova, Jeremy Blanton, Jean-Pierre Bonnefous, Michel Canesi, Hélène Ciolkovitch, Florence Clerc, Rudi van Dantzig, Yelena Demikovsky, Jeanette Etheredge, Lorna Geddes, Maude Gosling, Vanessa Harwood, Jane Hermann, Rashna Homji, Stephen Jeffries, Anna Kisselgoff, Charles Jude, Natasha Harley, Karen Kain, Martin Kamer, Tessa Kennedy, Charles Kirby, Irina Kolpakova, Andre Larquié, Toby Leibovitz, Murray Louis, Gloria Luoma, Francis Mason, Monica Mason, Tatiana Massine, Marie-Christine Mouis, Mikko Nissinen, Luigi Pignotti, Nadia Potts, Elaine Rawlings, Tomas Schramek, Nancy Sifton, Diane Solway, Sergiu Stefanschi, Veronica Tennant, Sir John Tooley, Sharon Vanderlinde, and Barry Weinstein.

The writers who have come before me, with their insightful books and articles about Rudolf. In particular, I recommend for further reading the books written by Clive Barnes, John Percival, and Alexander Bland (although some may be out of print, you can find them in a library), and Diane Solway for adult readers. To young readers, I especially recommend Rudolf's autobiography, which was written with Alexander Bland (Nigel and Maude Gosling). To me, it is a treasured piece of history because it captures Rudolf's feelings and impressions as a young dancer. To Maude Gosling, I offer a special thank-you for allowing me to use quotes from that book.

Finally, to family and friends who have offered wise and loving counsel or help throughout this long process, including my wonderful in-laws, Grenville and Ethel Alguire; my brother, Gary, and sister-in-law, Sharon; my children, Michael, Cameron, and Alexandra; David Allan; Alan Cooper; Russel Daniel; Elaine Danson; Adele Deacon; Lois and Richard Dodds; Christopher Fleming; Millicent Jones; Maria Luisa Lamang; Jennifer Levere; Kim MacArthur; Christine McClendon; Les Petriw; Barbara Riggins; Earle Taylor; Denise Shenkman-Zarn; Michael Shenkman; and especially to my husband, Bill Alguire, who broke my fear of the first blank page by advising, "Just start writing, write from the heart, and the rest will take care of itself."

PHOTO CREDITS

Courtesy of the Alguire family: 121; 124 (top left, top right, bottom left); American Ballet Theatre Foundation: 154; Myra Armstrong: 86, 127 (top); courtesy of the Bali family: 124 (middle right); courtesy of Marika Besobrasova: 165; Anthony Crickmay: 6, 72, 90; Mike Davis (with the permission of Jesse Davis): 66; Erik Dzenis: 10, 96, 98, 145; Beverley Gallegos: 134 (bottom); courtesy of Maude Gosling: 80; Ted Griffiths: 114; Walter Healy: 124 (middle center); © The Jim Henson Company: 138; courtesy of the Jude family: 124 (middle left, bottom right); courtesy of Tessa Kennedy: 124 (bottom center); from the Marilyn J. La Vine Collection, Library of Congress, Washington, D.C.: 70, 159; courtesy of Tobias Leibovitz: 83, 94, 171; Dina Makarova: 105; Jack Mitchell: 77, 157; Jacques Moatti: 167, 170; courtesy of the National Ballet of Canada: 140; courtesy of the Nureyev family: 16, 21 (left and right), 26, 28, 29, 30, 36; Louis Peres: 89, 109, 111, 120, 127 (bottom right), 134 (top right), 179; Michael Peto: 81; Bill Reilly: 142, 150; Roy Round: 127 (bottom left), 152; R. Torette: 118; Toronto Star: 174; V&A Picture Library: 20; Jack Vartoogian: 101; Linda Vartoogian: 130, 134 (top left); courtesy of Tamara Zakrzhevskaya: 2, 40, 46, 47, 48, 54, 58, 61, 68; Hector Zaraspe: 8, 37.

Additional thanks to the members of the Paris Opéra House publicity department and the National Ballet of Canada archive department.